PICTURING THE DPRK
북한을 그리다

GLYN FORD

PACIFIC CENTURY INSTITUTE

SPOKESMAN

Picturing the DPRK
by Glyn Ford

Introduction by Glyn Ford

© Glyn Ford 2023

First Published 2023 by Pacific Century Institute (PCI) and Spokesman Books

Photos and text © Glyn Ford unless otherwise noted
www.glynford.eu

Design, typeset, and image edits William Devereux
www.willdevphotography.co.uk

Text translation by Jackie Lee of PCI

Published and distrubuted (US and Asia) by
Pacific Century Insitute,
19850 Plummer Street,
Chatsworth,
CA 91311,
USA.
Tel. +1 (818) 721-5555
pci@pacificcenturyinst.org

Published and distrubuted (UK and Europe) by
Spokesman Books,
5 Churchill Park,
Nottingham,
NG4 2HF,
UK.
Tel. +44 (0)115 9708318
www.spokesmanbooks.org

A catalogue record is availible from the British Library.

All rights reserved. No part of this publication may be reproduced, stored in a retrieval system or transmitted in any form or by any means (electronic, mechancial, photocopying, recording or otherwise), without the prior permission of both the copyright owner and the above publishers of this book.

IBSN: 978 0 85124 926 1 Hardback
IBSN: 978 0 85124 927 8 Kindle

Printed in South Korea

10 9 8 7 6 5 4 3 2 1

PICTURING THE DPRK

North Korea, or as it prefers to be known, the Democratic People's Republic of Korea (DPRK), is portrayed as mysterious and malevolent with its leadership denounced for its military enterprise and human rights abuses. It is no one's poster boy for anything positive, prejudged as perennially guilty of the worst actions for the worst reasons. Yet, hidden behind this facade are the people of the DPRK. Outside the circle of family and friends who hold the reigns of power and feature so prominently in the coverage of the tabloids and TV, there are 26 million men, women and children like us. These millions have their hopes, dreams, and fears that march on a treadmill that rarely stops, save intercut with rest and play. *Picturing the DPRK* puts these people and their places centre stage. They, and the rest of the people on the Peninsula, will be the hapless victims of any attempt to force regime change or any inadvertent stumbling into war. The lessons of Iraq, Libya and Syria have taught the world that applied idealism in the absence of realism is the road to hell in a handcart. This prelude in epitome sets out the historical, social, and economic parameters within which they live their lives.

25 YEARS

I have been travelling to the DPRK now for more than a quarter of a century with close to fifty visits. In those years, I have criss-crossed the country from the Russian border to the Demilitarised Zone (DMZ) (301), from the mouth of the Yalu (627) to Kaesong (323), and from Nampo to Wonsan (348). The only lacunae are the central wedge north of Huichon and the stretch of coast between Sinp'o and Ch'ongjin. Apart from in Pyongyang, I have had close accompaniment on all my visits, most commonly by officials from the International Department of the Workers' Party of Korea. Was I limited in what I could observe? - Absolutely! Did I see what few others have seen? - Yes. I was even afforded the opportunity to observe a local election (108). For all this, pictures are far more eloquent than words.

RULED AND DIVIDED

Korea is a country divided by ruler. The instrument was called into service by Dean Rusk and Charles Bonesteel on 10 August 1945 when the Pacific war entered its endgame. They drew a straight line on a National Geographic map closely bisecting the Peninsula along the 38th parallel, carefully gifting Washington the capital, Seoul. Soviet ambitions were to be limited to the North, while the US was to be rewarded with the South. Yet, in the aftermath of the victory over Japan, the Korean people's desire to be one was manifest, but that destiny was diverted, subverted, and thwarted. The Peninsula's early skirmishes turned to insurrection before on 25 June 1950 becoming a full-blown civil war. Both sides, sequentially on the brink of defeat, widened the conflict first to America and the West, then countered with China and a proxy Soviet Union. It was an undeclared war between China and the US, fought on neutral territory. The North's Korean People's Army (KPA) and the South's battalions were pushed aside into supporting roles as the war bogged down in the stalemate and stench of trench warfare. After the death of Stalin an armistice was finally signed recognising a line of control that was, in effect, the 38th parallel starting point with an anti-clockwise twist. From that date, 27 July 1953, history's clock ran slow in the North. There, seventy years on, the war remains part of everyday life in schools (202), street furniture (115), monuments (118), museums (311), cigarettes, and 727 licence plates, all catalysed in the performance and spectacle of the Mass Games (720) and the staccato punctuation of anniversaries (312).

IF AT FIRST YOU DO SUCCEED

In the immediate aftermath it was the North's economy that was first to take-off. By the late fifties and early sixties, the drive away from fields to the mines (126), factories (333), and smelters (331) of Soviet-style industrialisation had the DPRK at the top of the communist class. Its fans ranged from Che Guevara, via America's Black Panthers, to Cambodia's Prince Norodom Sihanouk. For all that, it was an end, not a beginning. By the close of that decade, the Peninsula's world was turned upside down. The conjuncture of state capitalism with South Korean characteristics delivered by Park Chung-hee saw the South's economy take-off and soar. All the while the North's stalled as it failed to ignite the second stage transition from heavy to light industry, from capital goods to consumer goods; the great divergence had started.

SHORT WAR

The war's ending was as disjointed as its start. The fiery tail of the outlier guerrilla bands, left behind in the Taebaek Mountains, had been extinguished by the late fifties, and its political wing's clandestine agitation (505) shortly after. As Seoul's economy overtook on the inside lane in the late sixties, Kim Il Sung's response was the misdirection of the 'small' Korean War that ran from 1966 to 1969. Pyongyang learnt the lessons of North Vietnam's own civil war with Washington, but learnt them badly. North and South traded military adventurism, incursions, and infiltrators to the mutual culminating point of failure. Both sides preferred playing away. Seoul's 330,000 troops rotating in and out of Vietnam were matched - at a heavy cost - by Pyongyang, who dispatched pilots to fly MiG-15s and MiG-21s in the defence of Hanoi from 1967 to early 1969 (311). They also sent ground forces to learn the South's military tactics and disperse propaganda. One consequence of all this was the 1968 shambles with the capture of the USS Pueblo (504) near Wonsan. All the US' Korean interpreters were off in Saigon monitoring cockpit chatter between the North's pilots and unavailable to help manage the unfolding crisis.

LONG SEE-SAW

Kim Il Sung skilfully played Beijing and Moscow off against each other for the next two decades as relations see-sawed between them. Grants and loans, countertrading and friendship pricing allowed Pyongyang's economy to limp, trailing behind the burgeoning South's. It was the collapse of the Soviet Empire in 1989 that ultimately broke the North. Moscow abandoned Pyongyang to its own devices and Beijing switched from friendship pricing to demanding payment in hard currency. The conjunction of bad news and bad weather was a tipping point. Drought followed by floods destroyed crops and shrank yields across several years. The short decade of slow famine, known in the North as the Arduous March, started as Kim Il Sung departed. Kim died on 8 July 1994.

It was then that I visited the North for the first time. Children were wasted (412), the cupboards of the Public Distribution Service were bare (102) and hospitals lacked basic supplies and equipment (408). The infrastructure was generally in place, just the inputs were missing. Belatedly, the world rallied around, with acutely different levels of generosity filling the food gap (103). By 2004, the situation was back to a new spare subsistence. Kim Jong Il was obliged to reluctantly embrace the market. The economy stabilised and slowly grew, while the North made vain attempts to substitute Washington for Moscow on that see-saw. Kim Jong Un saw Beijing more as a problem than a solution. China will ensure the regime survives, but on short rations. Pyongyang wants diplomatic engagement, but preferably without denuclearization. The forward march can be slowed, or even halted, but there is no reverse gear to engage for the moment!

MARKET WITH EAST ASIAN CHARACTERISTICS

What Kim Jong Il tolerated, Kim Jong Un embraced. Nonetheless, at macro-level it was not the American free market capitalism, but its East Asian correction modelled on State-Owned Enterprises; *Chaebol* and *Zaibatsu*. The state carrier, Air Koryo, expanded into taxis and food and drink (314). At micro-level, it was Ministry, Military, and Party units in public-private partnerships trading, and supplying consumer services under the broad umbrella of the state. Those independent spirits - habitually women - who ventured alone in the markets (104) and *Jangmadang* were tolerated, provided they only survived rather than thrived. When these *Ronin* - masterless Samurai - traders made serious money and were tempted into conspicuous consumption, they were firmly put down and in place. Kim wanted an emerging middle class, but just not one outside the system. They were to be the regime's organic buttresses, not its bulldozers; they are to play defence, not offence.

HOME AND AWAY

Kim Jong Un was only too aware of the twin threats hanging over him. The lessons of the 'coloured revolutions' and kinetic regime change in Iraq and Libya were there during his period of apprenticeship to his father. Syria started during his probation. The answers were, and are, to keep the people who matter happy - code for those that live in Pyongyang - and develop a credible nuclear deterrent that threatens the mainland United States. With the megaphone voices demanding regime change turning their attention to the Peninsula after the farrago of the *dar al-Islam*, they only drove forward Pyongyang's nuclear weapons programmes and the technological imperative for smarter intercontinental ballistic missiles (ICBMs) to threaten Washington.

The domestic threat is being palliated at some cost. When I first went during the early stages of the 'Arduous March', there was an equal opportunity desolation and desperation. Everyone was, by and large, in the same boat. Since then, the Gini index has flown. Pyongyang now lives in a world apart. Inside the policed boundaries of the capital are the SUVs - with and without their 727 number plates - restaurants, entertainment, and illumination. Outside the wood-burning lorries (616), fitful deliveries of rations by the Public Distribution Service, never-ending work, and darkness.

DUAL ECONOMY

Back in 2012, I met with the then head of the International Department of the Party. He outlined the targets of the new plan - steel and coal, cement and funfairs. On the last, they have delivered. The Kaeson Youth Funfair (711) is central to the city, along with Rungrado Island Dolphinarium (707), and Munsu Water Park (704). There was even a beer festival on the banks of the Taedong (737). The suburbs see the Mirim Horse Riding Club (719) and, where the geographical imperative demands, the entertainment extends far outside the curtilage of Pyongyang with the Masikryong Ski Resort (734), package tours to Mount Kumgang (754), and ambitious plans for the Wonsan-Kalma beach resort.

The conundrum is that North Korea is not a developing state. It is an impaired and impeded Industrial State, subject to and suffering under the weight of sanctions and ideology. At the top, there is self-awareness. With an economy in the South fifty-times more powerful than at home, there is a recognition that early unification can only be assimilation. Its people are, at least, as hard-working, intelligent, and committed as those in the South. If the burden of sanctions was lifted, they believe the North's economy could see year-on-year double digit growth. In a generation, the two would at least share the same economic league.

WEAKNESS, NOT STRENGTH

There is the same level-headed practical realism with respect to the military stand-off and arms race between North and South. The world is in denial about the realities behind Pyongyang's drive for nuclear deterrence. Its reverse-engineered ICBM Programme and its clutch of nuclear tests are a demonstration of weakness, not strength; an answer to paucity rather than plenty. The image of the North as an irrational actor hell-bent on military adventurism and provocation is at odds with the concrete situation on the Peninsula. Yet, there are none so blind as those that cannot see. This persistent vision of Pyongyang remains imprinted in Western thinking despite a South transformed by the 1990's 'miracle on the Han River'.

STRENGTH, NOT WEAKNESS

Seoul and Pyongyang are ceaseless dance partners. The former's tiger economy transfigured a 'waif and stray' into a global player. In lockstep with its burgeoning GDP, there was a ratcheting up of its military budget that saw the South leapfrog - in parallel with its civilian advance - into one of the world's top ten military powers. In contrast, an economically marooned Pyongyang barely stayed afloat, sinking back into 45th place with a budget in real terms on par with its spending back in 2000. While at the turn of the millennium, the South outspent the North by a factor of just less than three ($13B to $4.9B), now the North's budget is more than eleven times smaller ($4.5B to $50.0B). To put it even more starkly, Seoul's increase in Defence spending in 2021 ($4.7B) exceeded the North's total military budget. Even in regional terms, there has been a changing of the guard. In 2001, Seoul's military budget of $13B was dwarfed by Tokyo's $41B. By 2021, it was nip and tuck as Seoul's $50B closed on Japan's $54B for the year.

But it is not just quantitative. Seoul has turned from 'taker to maker'; from buyer to supplier of military hardware. For decades, Seoul rang the tills and provided out-relief for the US military industrial complex, as it dutifully spent its military budget buying American. South Korean service personnel rode, flew, and sailed US haulage; outfitted and equipped with US small arms and heavy weapons. That all began to change as South Korea's Industrial Revolution started to trickle down into its own military industrial complex. Once started, there was no stopping.

The South's defence industry was preordained to build American by design with US-compatible weapons and equipment. After all, it was impossible then to imagine a South Korean road to war absent Washington. It started with the marginal, with the peripheral, but over the last decade, the South's weapons production has gone from homespun to export, with Seoul increasingly seeing itself as a major player in the global arms market. The sales pitch is now they can deliver NATO attuned military hardware faster, and at lower prices than the US. An attractive proposition as the West re-arms and re-stocks after Ukraine.

Seoul was already at number eight in the global arms market and has set a target to catch, and pass China, to secure fourth spot. In contrast, Pyongyang's last recorded arms exports were to Niger, El Salvador, and Trinidad and Tobago. From Pyongyang's perspective, it has been outmanned and outgunned by the Seoul-Tokyo-Washington triad for a half century. Pyongyang believed it was at least in the game with the credibility gap bridged by its national morale multiplier. The fate of Iraq, Libya, and Syria, and the march of time and technology have forced them to face the future. For in, a sense worse is to come, the same threat will be there - if it is not already - from a solitary South. The North already sees a quarter of its GDP swallowed by its military. Even a 'military first' policy must live in the real world.

MANPOWER AND ENERGY

The North's economy is broken on two rocks - energy and manpower. There are chronic energy shortages hampering the functioning of industry at all levels. The North's hydropower take is close to its natural limits, its coal industry tired, and in some cases close to exhaustion. Without dependence, the way forward for the hard baseload power to run large factories manned with cheap skilled labour, is a civil nuclear programme. This is why Kim, in Hanoi, was willing to give up the whole of the Yongbyon site, but not surrender his last uranium enrichment facility. The North's indigenous Light Water Reactors will run on its low enriched uranium. The reason why the North has taken umbrage at Biden's sleight of hand in unilaterally changing the Singapore Declaration's 'denuclearised Peninsula' to a 'denuclearised North Korea'. As the South has no intention of surrendering its civil nuclear programme, Singapore said yes to a civil nuclear programme in the North while the second puts that to the question.

GARRISON STATE

All roads lead to Rome. The reality that the country is an industrial, rather than developmental, state means there is no pool of peasant labour available to be inducted into the challenges and discipline of industrial society. Where are the men? In the Army. The KPA was/is a facsimile of the Soviet Union's Red Army writ small, with the same institutional structure and ethos. After Kim took back control in 1957 as Chinese troops left and the Sino-Soviet split tore Communism asunder, it was adapted and repurposed for the increasingly heterodox ideology of Kim Il Sung and his successors.

Its role in society has become the backbone of the country with soldiers serving as corvée labour for planting, harvesting, and prestige projects. Conscription, when introduced back in 1956, was three and a half years, yet had stretched to thirteen in the mid-90's and has now settled back on ten. The result is 1.2 million KPA soldiers and 600,000 reservists, close to a third of working age men. The military budget, as low as 3% of GDP in 1960, saw a sharp step change and has long since absorbed more than a quarter of the Nation's resources. All men are conscripted, save criminals and college students, the ill and the 'hostile'. Until recently, few resisted, with army life the easier option; now, for some, the market calls.

HOBSON'S CHOICE

The only answer that matches the North's purse, maintains a deterrent against any kinetic ventures by Seoul or Washington, decants hundreds of thousands of KPA soldiers into the labour market and fills the energy gap, is the nuclear one. Kim effectively indicated as much in his 2019 New Year's Address. Thus, Seoul and Washington are the inadvertent architects of the North's nuclear deterrent and ICBM programmes. The fact is, the only narrow path offering answers to Pyongyang's twin domestic and international dilemmas, is the nuclear. The North has no choice but to become a Batesian mimic - adopting the dress and deployment of a predator - and count on perception to override the reality of its inability to adequately arm itself with conventional weapons. This makes the North more dangerous, not less. Demonising its people only reinforces jeopardy. With its conventional forces outgunned by Seoul - let alone with Washington and Tokyo - the ladder of escalation has only two rungs before catastrophe faces the people of the Peninsula and Northeast Asia. War is then an accident waiting to happen.

All photographs seen in this photobook are of Pyongyang unless otherwise stated.

001   *Cover image* - A day out at the beach, Wonsan. (2012)

002   *Blurb image* - Meeting with Ri Su Yong, Vice-President of Politburo Executive and Head of International Department of Worker's Party of Korea (2016-20). Image © 2012 KCNA

북한을 그리다

북한 또는 당사자들이 선호하는 명칭인 조선민주주의인민공화국(DPRK)은 불가해하고 악한 곳으로 그려지며 지도부는 군사 행위와 인권 유린으로 비난을 받는다. 늘 최악의 이유로 최악의 행동을 한다는 예단을 받으며 아무도 북한을 긍정적인 모범으로 내세우지 않는다.

그러나 그 이면에는 북한 국민들이 숨겨져 있다. 권력을 장악하고, 선정적 매체와 TV 보도에 아주 요란하게 등장하는 일가와 추종자들의 세계 밖에는 우리와 같은 2,600만 명의 남성, 여성, 어린이가 있는 것이다. 간간이 끼어 있는 휴식과 오락 시간을 제외하고는 이 수백만 명의 희망, 꿈, 두려움은 거의 쉬지 않고 행진 중이다. 북한을 그리다는 그런 사람들과 그들이 있는 장소를 무대 중앙에 올리고 있다. 그들과 한반도의 나머지 사람들은 어떤 강제적인 정권 교체 시도나 부주의로 어쩌다 전쟁에 빠지는 일이 있을 경우 불운한 희생자들이 될 것이다. 이라크, 리비아, 시리아의 교훈은 현실주의 없이 이상주의를 적용하는 것은 손수레를 타고 지옥으로 가는 길이라는 것을 세계에 가르쳤다. 이 서문은 그들이 삶을 살고 있는 역사적, 사회적, 경제적 조건들을 요약하여 제시하고자 한다.

25 년

나는 25 년 이상 동안 북한을 거의 50회 여행했다. 그 세월 동안 나는 러시아 국경에서 비무장지대(DMZ)까지(301), 압록강 하구에서(627) 개성까지(323), 남포에서 원산까지(348) 전국을 누볐다. 빠진 지역은 희천 북쪽의 중앙 쐐기대와 신포-청진간 해안 뿐이다. 평양을 제외하고는 모든 곳을 방문할 때 밀착 동행자가 있었으며 대부분 조선로동당 국제부 관리들이었다. 내가 뭘 볼 수 있는지 제한을 받았을까? 당연히 그랬다! 나는 다른 사람들이 본 적이 거의 없는 것들을 보았나? 그랬다. 나는 지방선거를 참관할 기회까지 얻었다(108). 이 모든 이유로 그림은 말보다 훨씬 더 많은 것을 말해준다.

통치와 분단

한국은 통치자에 의해 분단된 나라이다. 그 도구는 1945년 8월 10일 태평양 전쟁이 막바지에 이르렀을 때 Dean Rusk와 Charles Bonesteel에 의해 사용되었다. 그들은 내셔널 지오그래픽 지도에 38도선을 따라 직선을 그어 한반도를 면밀하게 양분하며 수도 서울은 세심하게 워싱턴에 선사했다. 소련의 야망은 그 북쪽으로 제한되었고 미국은 남쪽으로 보상을 받았다. 하지만 일본 패전 후 한민족의 하나되고자 하는 염원이 명백했음에도 불구하고 그들의 운명은 방향이 전환되고, 전복되고, 좌절되었다. 한반도 양측의 초기 충돌들은 1950년 6월 25일 본격적인 전쟁이 되기 전에 봉기로 바뀌었다. 양측은 각자 패망에 직면하자 처음에는 미국과 서방으로 분쟁을 확대했고 그 다음에는 중국과 소련 대리군으로 반격했다. 이는 중국과 미국 사이의 선전포고 없는 전쟁이었고, 중립 구역에서 싸운 것이었다. 전쟁이 참호전의 악취와 교착상태에 빠지자 북한의 조선인민군과 남한의 군대는 지원 역할로 밀려났다. 스탈린이 사망한 후 마침내 휴전 협정이 체결되며 시계 반대 방향으로 꼬인 38선이 사실상 시작되었다. 1953년 7월 27일 그날부터 북한에서 역사의 시계는 느리게 흘러갔다. 70년이 지난 지금도 그곳에서는 전쟁이 학교(202), 거리 장식(115), 기념물(118), 기념관(311), 담배와 727이 들어간 자동차 번호판 등을 통해 일상 생활의 일부로 남아 있으며, 화려한 매스게임(720) 공연과 짧고 강렬한 기념일들이(312) 그 모든 것들에 대한 촉매작용을 한다.

처음에 성공했지만

전쟁 직후 먼저 도약한 것은 북한 경제였다. 50년대 후반과 60년대 초반에 이르러 농지에서 광산(126), 공장(333), 제련소(331)로 돌진하는 소련식 산업화 덕분에 북한은 공산주의 국가 중 최상위 반열에 올랐다. 북한 팬은 체 게바라로부터 미국의 블랙팬서, 캄보디아의 노로돔 시아누크공에 이르기까지 다양했다. 그 모든 것에도 불구하고 그것은 시작이 아니라 끝이었다. 그 10년이 끝날 무렵 한반도의 세상은 완전히 뒤집혔다. 박정희 대통령이 국가자본주의를 남한의 특성과 결합시키는 정책을 폄으로써 남한 경제는 비약했다. 그러는 동안 북한은 중공업에서 경공업으로, 자본재에서 소비재로 가는 제 2단계 전환에 점화하지 못하면서 주춤했고, 양측은 크게 갈리기 시작했다.

짧은 전쟁

전쟁의 결말은 시작만큼이나 혼란스러웠다. 태백산맥에 남겨졌던 고립된 게릴라 집단의 맹렬한 꼬리는 50년대 후반에 소탕되었고, 얼마 지나지 않아 그 정파의 비밀 선동(505)도 소멸되었다. 60년대 후반 서울의 경제가 북한을 추월하자 김일성의 대응은 잘못된 방향으로 흘러 1966년부터 1969년까지 '소규모' 한국전쟁이 진행됐다. 평양 당국은 북베트남이 미국과 벌인 내전에서 교훈을 얻었지만 잘못 배웠다. 남북한은 군사적 모험주의, 습격, 잠입 요원을 서로 주고받으며 피차 실패의 절정에까지 이르렀다. 양측 모두 원정 경기를 선호했다. 남한은 33만 명의 병력을 베트남에 교대 파병했고, 북한은 무거운 대가를 치르며 1967년부터 1969년 초까지 하노이 항어를 위해 MiG-15와 MiG-21을 비행할 조종사들을 파견하는 것으로 응수했다(311). 그들은 또한 남한의 군사 전술을 알아내고 선전을 퍼뜨리기 위해 지상군을 파견했다. 이 모든 것의 결과 중 하나는 1968년 원산 근처에서 USS 푸에블로(504)를 나포할 때 벌어진 혼란이었다. 미국의 모든 한국어 통역사들은 사이공에서 북한 조종사들 간의 조종석 대화를 감시하고 있느라고 전개되고 있는 이 위기를 관리하는 데 도움을 줄 수 없었다.

긴 시소 게임

김일성은 그후 20년 동안 중국과 소련의 관계가 시소 게임 양상을 보이는 가운데 양국을 능숙하게 요리했다. 북한은 급성장하는 남한 경제에 뒤처진 채 보조금과 차관, 대응 무역, 우호 가격 등을 통해 지지부진한 상태를 이어갈 수 있었다. 결국 북한를 무너뜨린 것은 1989년 소비에트 제국의 붕괴였다. 소련은 알아서 살도록 북한을 포기했고 중국은 우호 가격에서 경화 지불을 요구하는 쪽으로 전환했다. 나쁜 소식에 나쁜 날씨까지 결합된 것이 티핑 포인트였다. 가뭄 뒤에 홍수가 따라오면서 농작물을 망가뜨렸고 수 년 동안 수확량이 줄게 만들었다. 북한에서 고난의 행군으로 알려진 10년간의 지리한 기근은 김일성이 떠나며 시작되었다. 김일성은 1994년 7월 8일 사망했다.

내가 처음으로 북한을 방문한 것이 바로 그 때였다. 아이들은 쇠약해 있었고(412), 정부 배급소 창고는 텅 비어 있었고(102), 병원에는 기본 물품과 장비가 부족했다(408). 기반시설은 대체로 갖춰져 있었는데 단지 그곳에 투입할 물자가 없는 거였다. 뒤늦게 전세계가 나서 식량

부족을 채웠는데 후한 정도는 각국이 뚜렷한 편차를 보였다(103). 2004년쯤 되자 상황은 새로이 근근이 먹고사는 수준으로 돌아갔다. 김정일은 마지못해 시장을 받아들일 수 밖에 없었다. 경제는 안정되며 서서히 성장했고, 북한은 시소 상대를 러시아에서 미국으로 대치하려는 헛된 시도를 했다. 김정은은 중국 정부를 해결책이라기보다는 문제로 보았다. 중국은 정권 생존을 보장하겠지만 배급 식량이 부족할 터였다. 평양은 외교관계를 원하지만 비핵화 없이 그러기를 바란다. 앞으로 가는 행진은 늦추거나 심지어 멈출 수도 있지만, 후진 기어는 현재 없다!

동아시아 특성을 가진 시장

김정일은 그냥 눈감아줬던 것을 김정은은 포용했다. 그럼에도 불구하고 거시적 차원에서 그것은 미국의 자유시장 자본주의가 아니라 한국과 일본의 재벌과 같은 중국 국유 기업을 모델로 한 동아시아 수정판이었다. 국영 항공사인 고려항공은 택시, 음식, 음료(314)로 사업을 확장했다. 미시적 차원에서 이는 정부 부처, 군 및 당 단위부서들이 공공-민간 파트너십 거래를 하고 광범위한 국가 산하에서 소비자 서비스를 공급하는 거였다. 시장과 장마당에 홀로 과감히 나선 (104)독립적인 사람들(주로 여성)은 번창하지 않고 그저 생존하는 수준인 한 용인되었다. 영주 없는 사무라이인 이 낭인 상인들이 상당한 돈을 벌고 과소비 유혹에 넘어가면 그들은 단호히 제제를 받고 분수를 알게 되었다. 김은 신흥 중산층을 원했지만 그들이 제도권 밖에서 생기는 것은 원치 않았다. 그들은 정권의 유기적 지지대가 되어야지 불도저가 돼서는 안 되는 거였다. 그들은 공격이 아니라 방어를 해야 한다.

국내외 위협

김정은은 자신이 직면한 두 가지 위협을 너무 잘 알고 있었다. 이라크와 리비아의 '색깔 혁명'과 역동적 체제 변화의 교훈은 그가 아버지 밑에서 후계자 훈련을 받던 시절에 일어났다. 시리아 사태는 그가 아직 지도자 실습기간 중일 때 시작되었다. 해답은 중요한 사람들 (즉, 평양에 사는 사람들) 을 계속 행복하게 해주고 미국 본토를 위협하는 믿을 만한 핵 억지력을 개발하는 것이었다. 이슬람 나라들에서의 난장판 이후 정권교체 요구 확성기 역할을 하는 이들이 한반도로 관심을 돌리면서 그들은 단지 북한의 핵무기 프로그램과 워싱턴을 위협할 더 고기능 대륙간탄도미사일(ICBM) 기술의 절박한 필요성을 촉진시켰을 뿐이다.

국내 위협은 얼마간의 대가를 치르며 완화되고 있다. 내가 고난의 행군 초기에 처음 북한에 갔을 때는 누구를 막론하고 모두 황폐하고 절박한 상태였다. 대개 모든 사람들이 한 배를 타고 있었던 것이다. 그 이후로 경제적 불평등 지수인 지니 지수는 치솟았다. 평양은 이제 완전히 다른 세상에 살고 있다. 치안이 유지되는 수도 경계 안에는 고위 관리를 위한 727번호판이 달리거나 안 달린 SUV, 레스토랑, 오락과 조명이 있다. 그 바깥 세상에는 장작을 연료로 쓰는 트럭(616), 배급소의 변덕스런 식료품 공급, 끝없는 노동, 그리고 어둠이 있다.

이중 경제

2012년에 나는 당시 당 국제부장을 만났다. 그는 철강과 석탄, 시멘트, 유원지 등 새로운 계획의 목표를 설명했다. 그들은 계획 중 마지막

항목을 이행했다. 개선청년공원(711)은 능라도의 평양 곱등어관(707), 문수물놀이장(704)과 함께 도시의 중심이다. 대동강변에서 맥주축제까지 열리기도 했다 (737). 교외에는 미림승마구락부 (719)가 있으며, 지리적으로 적소인 곳에는 오락 기회가 평양의 경계에서 훨씬 벗어난 곳까지 연장되어 마식령 스키장(734), 금강산 패키지 여행과(754) 함께 원산갈마 해안관광지구에 대한 야심찬 계획도 있다.

난제는 북한이 개발도상국이 아니라는 데 있다. 그들은 제재와 이념의 무게 하에 시달리며 망가지고 장애를 겪는 산업 국가이다. 최고 지도부는 자각하고 있다. 남한의 경제력이 자기들보다 50배나 더 강한 만큼 조기 통일은 상대에 동화하는 것일 뿐이라는 인식디 있다. 북한 국민들은 적어도 남한 사람들단큼 근면하고 영리하며 헌신적이다. 제재의 부담이 풀리면 북한 경제가 해마다 두 자릿수 성장을 할 수 있다고 그들은 믿는다. 한 세대만 지나면 양측이 적어도 같은 경제수준 범주에 속하게 될 것이라고.

강한 게 아니라 약한 북

남북간 군사적 대치와 군비경쟁에 대해서도 같은 냉정한 현실주의가 존재한다. 세계는 북한의 핵 억지력 추진 뒤에 숨은 현실을 부정하고 있다. 북한의 분해 모방을 통한 ICBM 프로그램과 핵실험은 그들의 힘이 아니라 약함을 드러낸다. 그것은 넉넉함보다는 부족함에 대한 해답인 것이다. 군사적 모험과 도발에 몰두하는 비이성적 행위자라는 북한의 이미지는 한반도의 구체적 정세와 상충된다. 그러나 보지 못하는 사람만큼 눈먼 사람도 없다. 남한이1990년대 '한강의 기적'으로 변모했음에도 불구하고 평양에 대한 이 끈질긴 환상은 서구 사고에 각인되어 있다.

약한 게 아니라 강한 남

남북한은 지속적인 댄스 파트너이다. 남한의 호랑이 경제는 '천애고아'를 글로벌 플레이어로 탈바꿈시켰다. 급증하는 GDP에 발맞춰 국방예산이 민간 경제 발전과 병행해 증가하며 남한은 세계 10대 군사 강국 중 하나로 도약했다. 이와는 대조적으로 경제적으로 궁지에 몰린 북한은 겨우 떠있는 상태로 45위로 추락했으며 국방 예산의 실질 가치는 2000년 지출액과 동일하다. 밀레니엄 전환기에 남한은 북한의 3배에 약간 못 미치게 (130억 글러 대 49억 달러) 지출했지만, 이제 북한의 예산은 남한보다 11배 이상 적다 (45억 달러 대 500억 달러). 더 극명하게 말하자면 2021년 남한의 국방예산 증액 금액 (47억 달러)이 북한의 국방예산 총액을 넘어섰다. 한반도 외 지역적으로도 경비대 교대가 이루어졌다. 2001년 남한의 국방예산 130억 달러는 일본의 410억 달러에 비하면 왜소했다. 2021년에는 남한의 500억 달러가 일본의 540억 달러에 근접하면서 막상막하가 되었다.

하지만 이는 단순히 양적인 것만이 아니다. 한국은 군수품의 '수취인에서 제조자로', 구매자에서 공급자로 변모했다. 수십 년 동안, 한국은 국방 예산을 착실하게 미국 제품을 사는 데 사용하면서 미국 방산업계에 보조금을 지불했다. 남한 군인들은 미제 소형 무기와 중화기로 장비, 장착된 미제 수송 수단들을 타고, 비행하고, 항해했다. 그 모든 것은 한국의 산업 혁명이 방산업겨 로까지 미치면서 변하기 시작했다. 그리고 일단 시작되자, 멈출 줄 몰랐다.

남한의 방산업계는 미국 제품과 호환되는 무기와 장비를 갖춘 미국 설계 제품을 제조하도록 예정되어 있었다. 결국 미국 없이 한국이 전쟁에 이를 방법은 당시에는 상상조차 할 수 없었다. 한국의 무기 생산은 보잘것없는 주변기기로 시작됐지만 지난 10년 동안 자급자족에서 수출로 바뀌었고, 한국은 점점 더 자신들을 세계 무기시장의 선두주자로 여기고 있다. 이제 그들은 NATO 에 맞춘 군사 장비를 미국보다 더 저렴한 가격에 더 빠르게 제공할 수 있다고 내세우며 구매를 권유한다. 우크라이나 전쟁 후 서방이 재무장과 무기 재고 보충에 나선 가운데 이는 매력적인 제안이다.

한국은 이미 세계 무기 시장에서 8위였고 중국을 제치고 4위를 차지하겠다는 목표를 세웠다. 대조적으로, 마지막으로 기록된 북한의 무기 수출은 니제르, 엘살바도르, 트리니다드 토바고에 대한 거였다. 북한 입장에서는 반세기 동안 한-미-일 3국에 인력과 화력에서 밀려왔다. 북한은 국가 평판 격차에 대한 임시 해결책으로 국민 사기를 배가시키면 적어도 게임이 끝난 것은 아니라고 믿었다. 이라크, 리비아, 시리아의 운명, 그리고 시간과 기술의 행진은 그들로 하여금 미래를 직시하게 만들었다. 어떤 의미에서는 미래가 더 나쁠 것이기 때문이다. 독자적 남한의 위협이 이미 있는 게 아니라면 앞으로는 올 것이다. 북한은 이미 국내총생산(GDP)의 1/4 을 군이 삼키고 있다. 그런데 '선군' 정치도 현실세계에서 살아야 한다.

인력과 에너지

북한 경제는 에너지와 인력이라는 두 암초에 걸려 망가졌다. 만성적인 에너지 부족은 전반적 산업 기능에 지장을 주고 있다. 북한의 수력발전은 자연적 한계에 가깝고 석탄 산업은 소진해 어떤 경우에는 고갈에 가깝다. 남에게 의존하지 않고 값싼 숙련 노동력으로 대규모 공장을 돌리기 위해 확실한 기본 소요 전력을 얻는 방법은 민간 원자력 프로그램이다. 이것이 김정은이 하노이에서 영변 부지 전부를 기꺼이 포기하겠다면서도 마지막 우라늄 농축 시설은 포기하지 않으려 한 이유이다. 북한 고유의 경수로는 저농축 우라늄으로 가동되게 된다. 이는 싱가포르 선언의 '비핵화된 한반도'를 '비핵화된 북한'으로 일방적으로 바꾼 바이든의 교묘한 속임수에 북한이 분노한 이유이기도 하다. 남한이 민간 원자력 프로그램을 포기할 의사가 없기 때문에 싱가포르 선언은 북한의 민간 원자력 프로그램을 허용했는데 미국이 말을 바꾸면서 그것을 의문시하게 만든 것이었다.

병영 국가

모든 길은 로마로 통한다. 국가가 개발도상국이 아니라 산업 국가라는 현실은 산업 사회의 도전과 훈련에 투입할 수 있는 농민 노동력이 없다는 것을 의미한다. 남자들은 다 어디에 있을까? 군대에 있다. 조선인민군은 소련 붉은 군대와 동일한 제도적 구조와 정신을 가진 축소 복사판이었고 현재도 그렇다. 1957년 중국군이 떠나고 김일성이 다시 정권을 잡은 후, 중-소 분열이 공산주의를 쪼개 놓자 군은 점점 더 김일성과 그 후계자들의 이단적 이데올로기를 위해 개조되고 용도변경되었다.

군이 사회에서 국가의 중추 역할을 하게 되며 군인들은 파종, 수확 및 명망 있는 프로젝트를 위한 부역 노동에 복무하게 되었다. 징병

복무기간은 1956년 도입될 당시에는 3년 반이었지만 90년대 중반에는 13년으로 늘어났고 지금은 10년으로 정착됐다. 그 결과, 정규군 120만 명과 예비군 60만 명을 합치면 전체 노동 연령 남성의 1/3 에 가깝다. 1960년 GDP의 3%에 불과했던 국방예산은 급격한 변화를 겪었고 그 이후 오랫동안 국가 자원의 4분의 1 이상을 빨아들였다. 남자들은 범죄자와 대학생, 병자와 '적대자'를 제외하고는 모두 징집된다. 군대 생활이 더 편안한 선택이라 최근까지 이에 저항하는 사람이 거의 없었는데 이제 일부에게는 시장이 부르고 있다.

홉슨의 선택

북한의 주머니 사정에 맞고, 남한이나 미국의 적극적 모험에 대한 억지력을 유지하고, 수십만 명의 인민근을 노동 시장으로 내보내며 에너지 부족을 메우는 유일한 해결책은 핵무기이다. 김 위원장은 2019년 신년사에서 사실상 이를 시사했다. 따라서 남한과 미국은 북한의 핵 억지력과 ICBM 프로그램의 의도치 않은 설계자인 셈이다. 북한의 대내외적 이중 딜레마에 해답을 제공하는 옹색한 길은 핵 밖에 없는 것이 사실이다. 북한은 재래식 무기로는 충분히 무장할 수 없는 현실을 무시하기 위해 포식자의 복장과 전열을 취하고 감각에 의존하는 베이츠 의태꾼이 될 수밖에 없다. 이는 북한을 덜 위험하게 만드는 것이 아니라 더 위험하게 만든다. 북한 사람들을 악마화 하는 것은 위험을 강화시킬 뿐이다. 북한이 미국과 일본은 고사하고 남한에게도 재래식 전력에서 압도당하고 있는 상황에서 한반도와 동북아 사람들에게 닥칠 재앙으로 올라가는 사다리는 이제 계단이 두 개 밖에 남지 않았다. 그러면 전쟁은 언제든 일어날 수 있는 사고인 셈이다.

본서에서 별도로 장소 표시가 없는 사진은 모두 평양에서 촬영됐음.

001   Cover image – 해변에서의 하루, 원산. (2012)

002   조선로동당 정치국 중앙위원회 부위원장, 국제부 부장을 역임한 (2016-20) 리수용과의 회의. 사진 © 조선중앙통신사, 2012.

Daily Life
일상생활

101   *Previous Page* - Rehearsing in Kim Il Sung Square in the face of the Grand People's Study House. (2018)

전 페이지 - 인민대학습당 앞 김일성광장에서 연습 중.

102   *Left* - The Public Distribution Service delivering rations. After the 'Arduous March' in the late 1990's Koreans were increasingly dependent on the *Jangmadang* of private street stalls and markets. (2003)

좌 - 식량을 배급하고 있는 식량보급소. 1990년대 후반 고난의 행군 이후 북한인들은 점점 더 장마당 사설 노점과 시장에 의존하게 되었다.

103   *Right* - EU food aid. (1997)

우 – 유럽연합 식량 원조물자.

104 Tongil Market with over 2000 vendors selling everything from dog to dresses. (2005)

2000개 이상의 노점상들이 개부터 옷까지 모든 것을 파는 통일시장.

105 Kiosk Capitalism. (2003)
노점상 자본주의.

106 *Left* - Life goes on for those not rehearsing. (2011)

좌- 연습 중이 아닌 사람들은 일상으로.

107 *Right* - West Pyongyang `Thermal Power Plant. Soviet built in 1961. (2003)

우 - 서평양화력발전소. 1961년 소련이 건설.

108 & 109 *Lets all vote Yes!* Local Election Day 24 July 2011.

모두 다 찬성투표하자! 2011년 7월 24일 지방선거일.

110   Polling Clerks. (2011)
투표관리원.

111   Ballot Papers.
   투표지.

112   Polling booth.
   투표 부스.

114   Ri Ung Gil, International Department of the Workers' Party of Korea and interpreter. (2008)

조선로동당 국제부의 리웅길과 통역관.

113   Display of contributors at the base of Juche Tower. (2018)

주체탑 받침대에 게시된 기부자 명단.

115 Sprucing up the Army banner in Kim Il Sung Square. (2008)
김일성광장에 군기 단장.

116 Lenin and Marx flanked the entrance to the Ministry of Foreign Trade on Kim Il Sung Square until 2014. They were removed for refurbishment. They are yet to return. (2003)

레닌과 마르크스는 2014년까지 김일성 광장의 대외무역성 입구 곁을 지키고 있었다. 그들은 보수를 위해 철거되었는데 아직 돌아오지 않았다.

118 The real thing. (2009)
   당 기념탑 실물.

117 'Mini-Pyongyang' with a miniature Party monument. (2013)
   당 기념탑의 축소판이 있는 '미니 평양'.

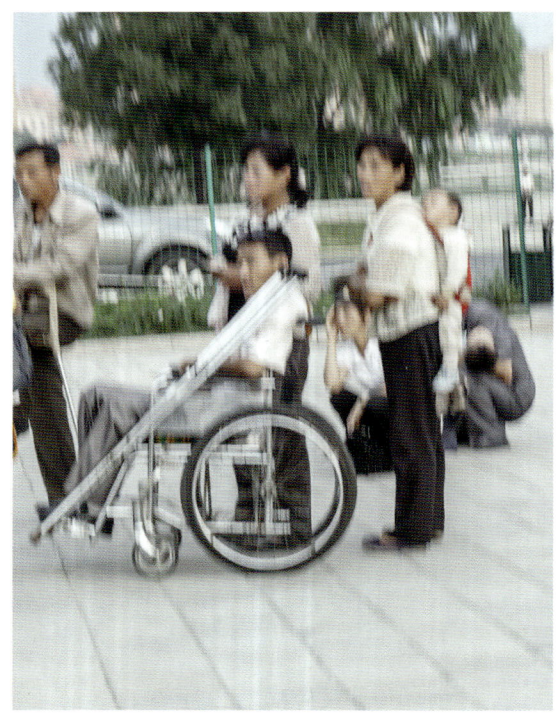

119 Despite claims to the contrary, disabled people can be seen on the streets of Pyongyang. (2013)

장애인이 없다는 주장에도 불구하고 평양의 거리에서는 장애인들이 보인다.

120   Talent decides everything.

121   *Top* - With the ideology and culture of the working class.
Bottom - Let's wipe out all the yellow culture of imperialism!

122   *Top* - Whoever invades our blue sky.
Bottom - Not a single one can survive!

123   Our Party's military-first politics is invincible!

124 (1998)

125 (2012)

126-128   Ryongmun Colliery. (1997)
룡문탄광.

129   Pit village off the Youth Hero Highway between Pyongyang and Nampo. (1998)

평양-남포간 청년영웅도로 변에 있는 탄광촌.

130   Changwang Street. (1997)

창왕거리.

131 *Left* - Hill Farming. (2012)
좌 - 산간농업.

132 *Right* - Crops heading to the market. (2011)
우 - 시장으로 가는 농작물.

From Nursery to University
교육, 유치원부터 대학까지

201 *Previous page* - Red-scarfed 'Young Pioneers' of the Korean Children's Union returning from rehearsals. (1998)

전 페이지 - 붉은 넥타이를 맨 조선소년단의 소년 피오네르(선구자)들이 리허설을 마치고 오는 중.

202 Defending the Nation against Japan and the United States. (2014)

일제와 미제에 대항하여 조국 수호.

203 War games for boy soldiers, Wonsan. (2014)
유년 군인들의 전쟁놀이, 원산.

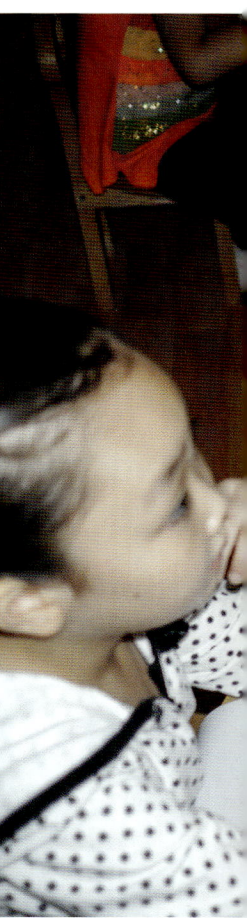

204 *Left* - Nursing girls. (2011)

좌 – 의사놀이 소녀들.

205 *Right* - Girls draw apples, boys fighter jets.

우 - 여학생은 사과를 그리고, 남학생은 전투기를 그리고.

206 Educational diorama of Mount Paektu, the birth place of Kim Jong Il. Haksan Cooperative Farm nursery school. (2008)
교육용 김정일의 백두산 생가 디오라마. 학산 협동농장 보육원.

207   Masundae, Birth place of Kim Il Sung.
김일성 성가.

208 Haksan Cooperative Farm nursery school. (2008)
학산 협동농장 보육원.

209 Wɔnsan model Children's Centre and Orphanage. (2014)
원산 모범아동센터 및 고아원.

211 A trip to Taesongsan Amusement Park. (1998)
대성산유희장(놀이공원) 나들이.

212　Wonsan. (2014)

원산.

213 *Left* - Mangyongade Children's camp. (2016)

좌 – 만경대소년단 야영소.

214 *Right* - Camp cookery.

우 – 야영소 주방.

215 Adding up. (2016)
덧셈 수업.

216 Hospital school. (2018)

병원내 학교.

217 *Left* - Embroidery academy. (2016)
좌 – 수예 학교. (2016)

218 *Right* - Tuning up at Pyongyang Music College.
우 - 평양음악대학에서 연습 중.

219   Kim Il Sung Univeristy halls of learning. (2013)
       김일성종합대학 학습관.

220   Study room at the Kim Il Sung University with posters urging the application of modern scientific techniques. (2016)

현대과학기술 활용을 촉구하는 포스터가 걸려 있는 김일성종합대학 교실.

221 Students at Kim Chaek University of Technology. (2011)

김책공업종합대학 학생들.

Fields, Factories, and Workshops
공사장, 공장, 작업장

301 *Previous page* - US military looking into the North at Panmunjom on the DMZ. (1997)

앞 페이지 - 비무장지대(DMZ) 판문점에서 북한 쪽을 들여다 보는 미군.

302 'Volunteers' building the Youth Hero Highway from Pyongyang to Nampo. (1998)

평양-남포간 청년영웅도로를 건설 중인 '자원봉사자'들.

303 Construction Workers. (2012)
건설 노동자들.

306　Ryongsong beer. (2011)
룡성맥주.

304　*Left* - Maintaining the image. (2009)
좌 – 벽화 관리.

305　*Right* - Raising the Nation's flag. (2011)
우 – 국기 게양.

71

307 *Left* - Yongmyongsa. (2011)

좌 - 용명사.

308 *Middle* - Russian Orthodox Church of the Life - Giving Trinity that opened in 2006. © 2008 Irina Kalashnikovav

중 - 2006년에 개설된 "생명을 주는 삼위일체" 러시아 정교희. © 2008년 이리나 칼라시니코바

309 *Right* - Pohyon Temple, Mount Myohyang. (2016)

우 - 묘향산 보현사.

310 A senior officer at the DMZ. (2012)

DMZ의 고위급 장교.

311 A display in the Fatherland Liberation War Museum, which opened in 2013, commemorating the pilots who died defending Hanoi between 1967-69 in dog-fights with US fighters. (2013)

2013년 개관한 조국해방전쟁승리기념관의 전시물. 1967년부터 1969년까지 하노이 방어를 위해 미국 전투기와 공중전을 벌이다 전사한 조종사들을 추모하는 전시물.

312 Waiting for Victory. Fatherland Liberation War commemoration, Hamhung. (27/07/2011)

승리를 기다리며. 조국해방전쟁승리 기념식, 함흥.

315   Air Koryo soft drinks. (2018)

고려항공 탄산수.

313   *Left* - Soldiers march at Mansu Hill Grand Monument. (2012)

좌 - 군인들이 만수대 대기념비에서 행진하고 있다.

314   *Right* - Loading processed fish for China, Rason. (2013)

우 - 중국행 가공처리 생선 선적, 라선시.

316 Rason Daehung Trading Corporation fish processing factory. (2012)
라선대흥무역회사 어류 가공공장.

317 Garment factory, Rason. (2012)
의류공장, 라선시.

318 'Snack' Factory control room. (2016)
'스낵' 공장 관제실.

320 *Left* - Making thread with a 'heroic' machine. Kim Jong Suk factory. (2009)

좌 – "영웅적" 기계로 실 제조 중, 김정숙 평양제사공장.

321 *Middle* - Kim Jong Suk Silk Mill. (2016)

중 - 비단실 제조, 김정숙 평양제사공장.

322 *Right* - Producing wiring harnesses for Korea's automobile industry in the Kaesong Industrial Complex. KIC was open between 2004-16 with over a hundred South Korean SMEs and 54,000 North Korean workers. (2012)

우 – 개성공단에서 한국 자동차업계용 와이어링 하네스 생산중. 개성공단은 2004년부터 2016년까지 가동됐으며 100개 이상의 남한 중소기업과 54,000명의 북한 근로자들이 참여했다.

319 Two workers operate a 'heroic' machine. (2009)

두 근로자가 또 다른 '영웅적' 기계와 함께.

323   Kaesong industrial complex. (2007)
개성공단.

326 Kaesong workers produce garments for the South Korean fashion company Shinwon. (2012)

개성 근로자들이 한국 패션기업 신원의 의류를 제조한다.

324 Toiletries produced in Pyongyang and Sinuiju Cosmetics Factory. (2014)

평양과 신의주 화장품 공장에서 생산되는 세면제품.

325 North Korean vodka, whiskey and 'adder' liquor. (2014)

북한 보드카, 위스키, '뱀' 술.

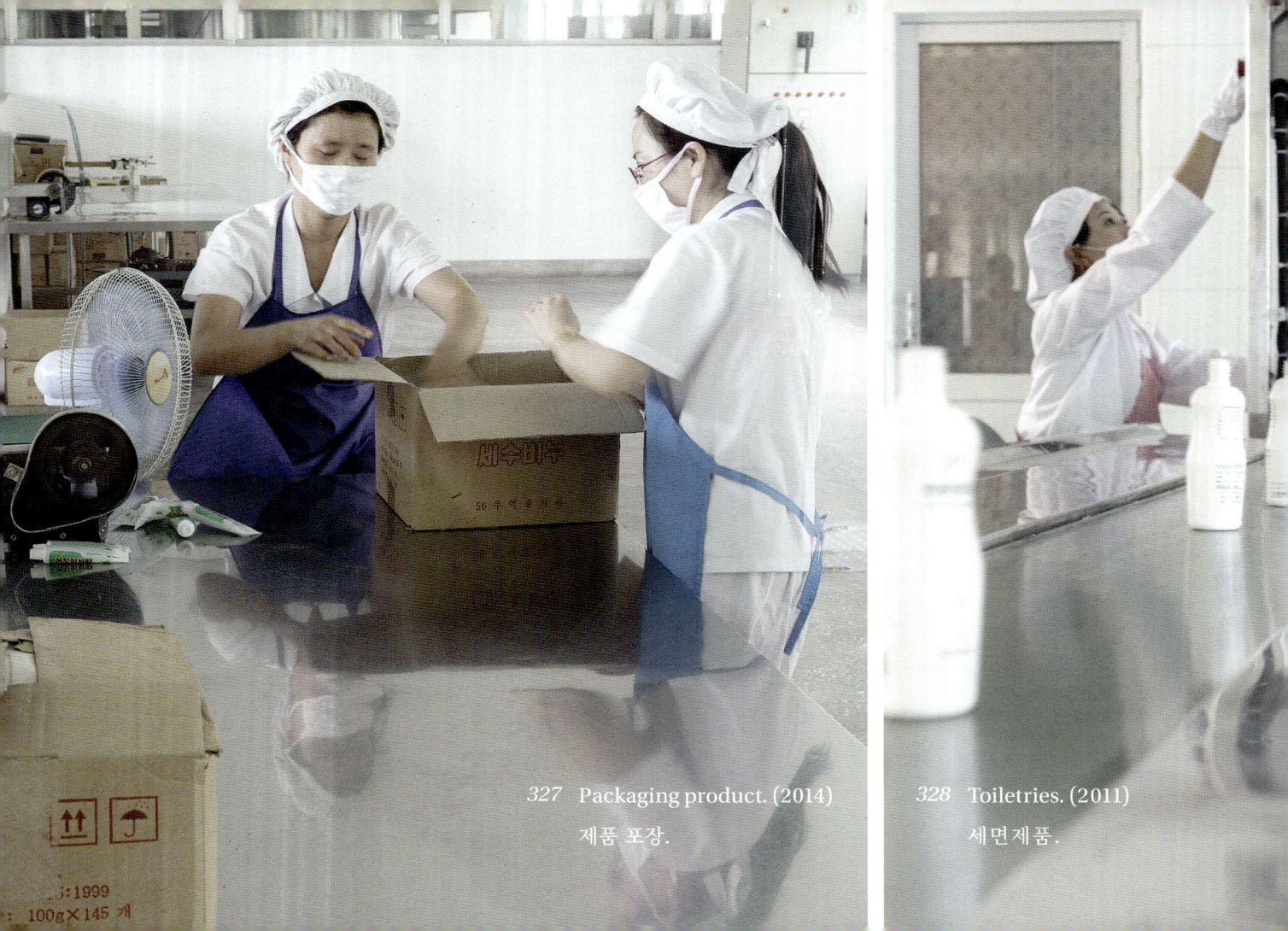

327 Packaging product. (2014)
제품 포장.

328 Toiletries. (2011)
세면제품.

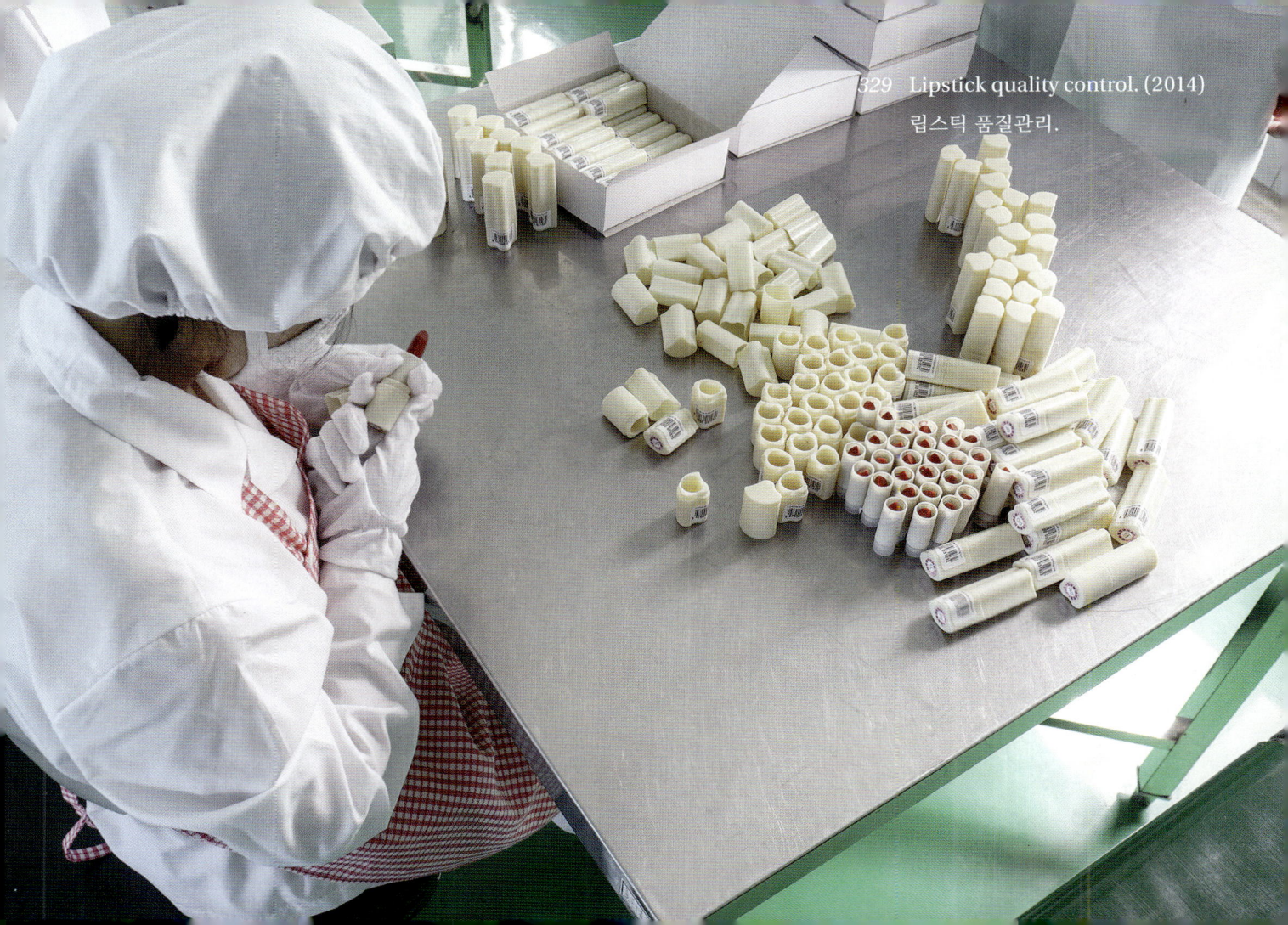

329 Lipstick quality control. (2014)
립스틱 품질관리.

330-331 Chollima Steelworks. (2009)
천리마 제철소.

332 *Left* - Chollima Steelworks. (2012)
좌 - 천리마 제철소.

333 *Right* - Lathe operator. (2012)
우 – 선반 기사.

334-335 European Union sponsored 'water shop' selling safe drinking water gravity fed from the mountains. (2011)

유럽 연합은 산에서 중력 방식으로 채수한 안전한 음용수를 판매하는 '생수 가게'를 후원했다.

336 Koryo Hotel Receptionist. (2012)
고려호텔 리셉셔니스트.

337 Masseuse. (2014)
마사지사.

338 Rason. (2012)
라선시.

339-340 **Left** - Ryugyong Hotel. Construction of this 330m 105 story hotel and business complex started in 1987 and was then suspended between 1992 until 2008. The exterior was finished in 2011. It is yet to open, but in 2018 graphic LED displays were added to light the night skies. (1997 and 2011)

좌 - 류경호텔. 330m 높이의 105층짜리 호텔과 비즈니스 단지 건축은 1987년에 시작되었고 1992년부터 2008년까지 중단되었다. 건물 외부는 2011년에 완성되었다. 아직 개장 전이지만 2018년에는 밤하늘을 밝히기 위해 그래픽 LED 전광판이 부착되었다.

341 **Right** - 'You're through to reception', Koryo Hotel. (2013)

우 - '리셉션 부분까지 완성', 고려호텔.

342 Cigarettes produced by the Naegohyang Tobacco Factory for export to Iran. (2016)

내고향 담배공장이 이란 수출용으로 생산한 담배.

343   Mowing the lawn. (2011)
       잔디 깎기.

344-345   Golden Triangle Bank, Rason. (2013)
황금의 삼각주 은행, 라선시.

346 Fresh shellfish, Wonsan Pier. (2012)
싱싱한 조개, 원산부두.

347 Street food - Wonsan style.
길거리 음식 - 원산 스타일.

348 Wonsan pier. For a small entry fee you use this tombolo to walk to the celebrated Jangdok island or fish for your supper. (2013)

원산부두. 약간의 입장료를 내면 이 섬 연결로를 이용해 유명한 장덕도로 가거나 저녁 찬거리로 생선을 낚을 수 있다.

349 Rural ox cart. Outskirts of Wonsan. (2012)
시골의 소달구지. 원산 외곽.

350 Ginseng farming, Kaesong. (2007)
인삼 농사, 개성.

351 Left - State farm near Pyongyang with a layout of the facility comprising of living quarters, recreational facilities, and farmland. (2014)

좌 – 평양 인근의 국영농장. 살림집, 여가시설, 농지로 구성되었다.

352 Middle - Scrumping apples from the Taedonggang Combined Fruit Farm. (2016)

중 – 대동강 과수종합농장에서 사과 서리.

353 Right - Farming terraces in Pongchon County. (2013)

우 – 봉천군 다락(계단식)밭.

In Sickness and Health
의료 서비스

401　*Previous page* - Under the blanket in Huichon's Children's Centre in the era of the 'Arduous March'. (1997)

전 페이지 - 고난의 행군 시절 희천탁아소에서 어린아이들이 이불을 덮고 있는 모습.

402　Pyongyang Maternity Hospital. To prevent infection, monitors are used between the new mother and family for the first weeks after birth. (2007)

평양산원. 감염 예방을 위해 출산 후 첫 몇 주 동안은 산모와 그 가족 간에 영상통화를 사용한다.

403 Remote diagnosis video link in Wonsan Provincial Hospital. Specialists in Pyongyang are able to diagnose patients across the country. The nurse caricature carries a magnolia, the state flower. (2013)

원산 도립 인민병원의 영상 연결 원격진단. 평양의 전문의들이 전국의 환자를 진단할 수 있다. 만화 속 간호사는 북한 국화인 함박꽃(모란)을 들고 있다.

404 Huichon hospital pathology lab. (1998)
희천병원 병리학 연구실.

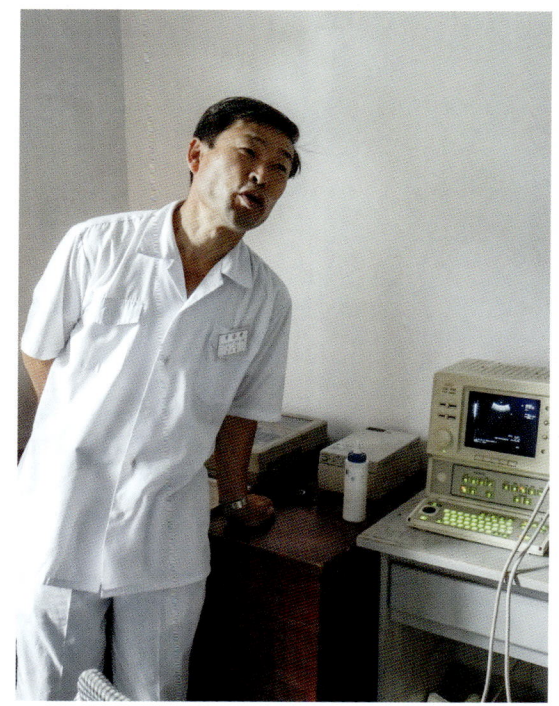

405 Ultrasound specialist in Pyongyang Maternity Hospital. (2012)

평양산원의 초음파 전문의.

406 State farm cottage hospital north of Pyongyang. (2011)

평양 북부 국영농장내 동네병원.

407 *Left -* Huichon Provincial Hospital ambulance. (1998)

좌 – 희천도립병원 구급차.

408 *Right -* 'Laboratory equipment'.

우 - '실험 장비'.

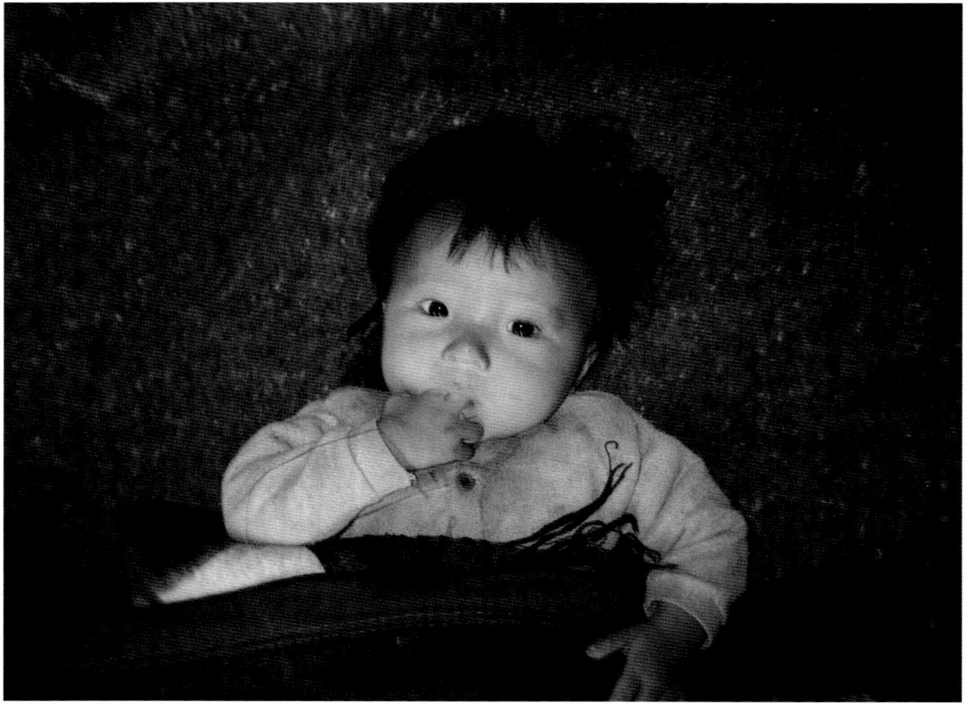

409-410 Sariwon Children's Centre. (1997)
사리원 탁아소.

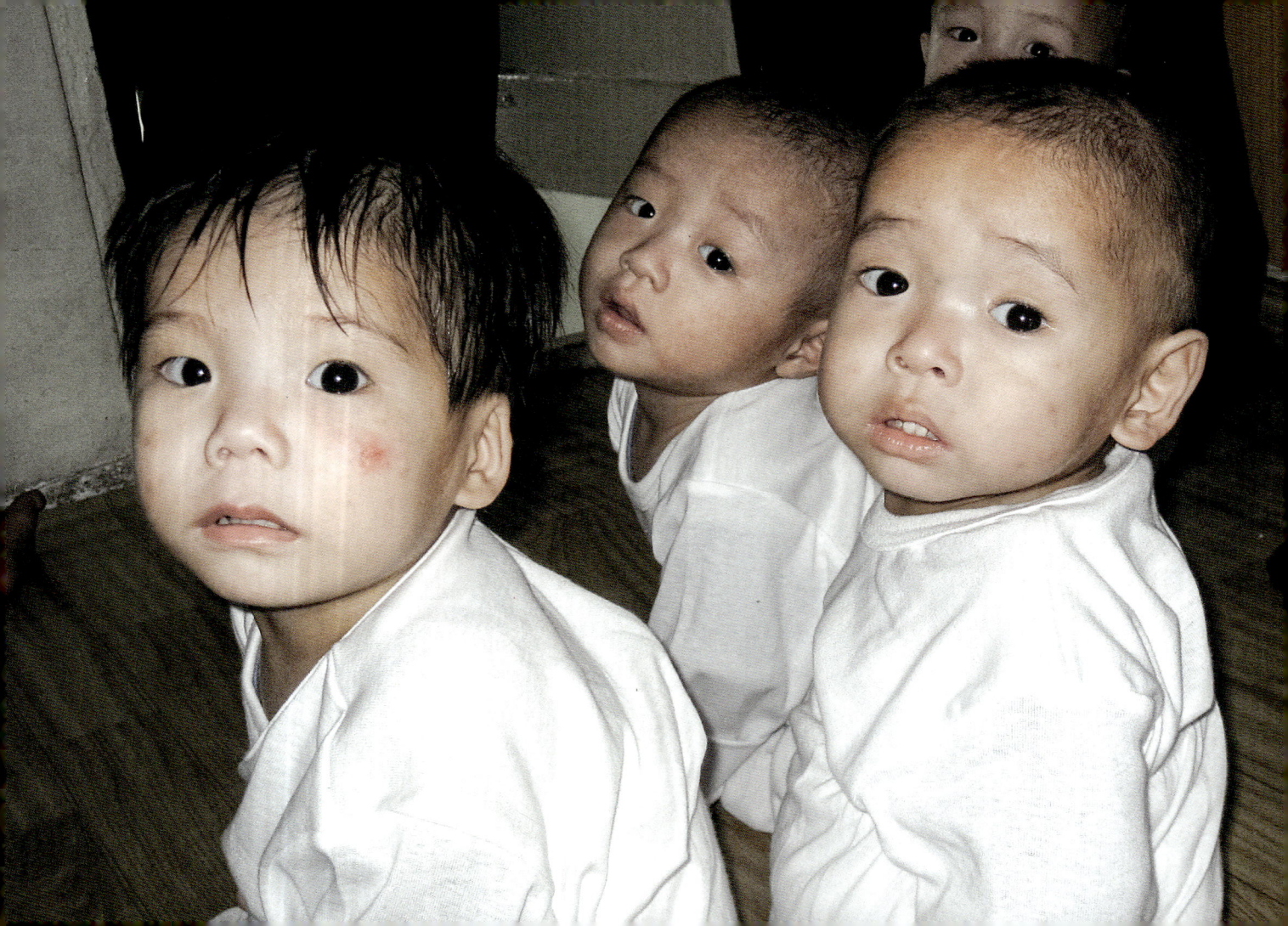

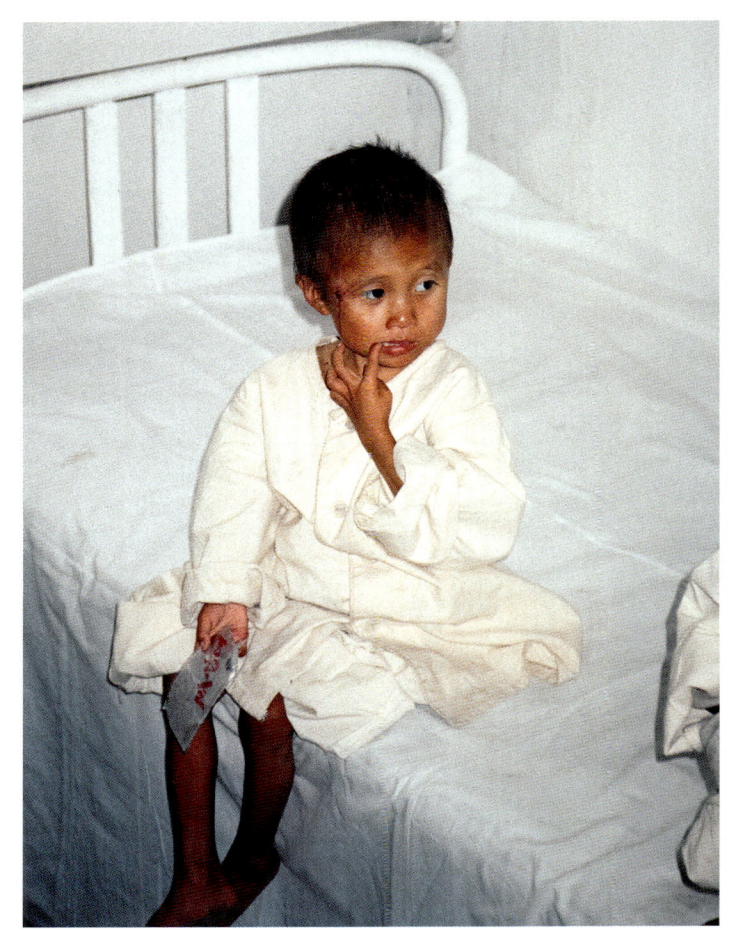

411   *Left* - Orphans at Majon Chilren's Centre. (2011)

좌 – 마전탁아소 고아들.

412   *Right* - A Children's Centre in Pyongyang. (1998)

우 - 평양 소재 탁아소.

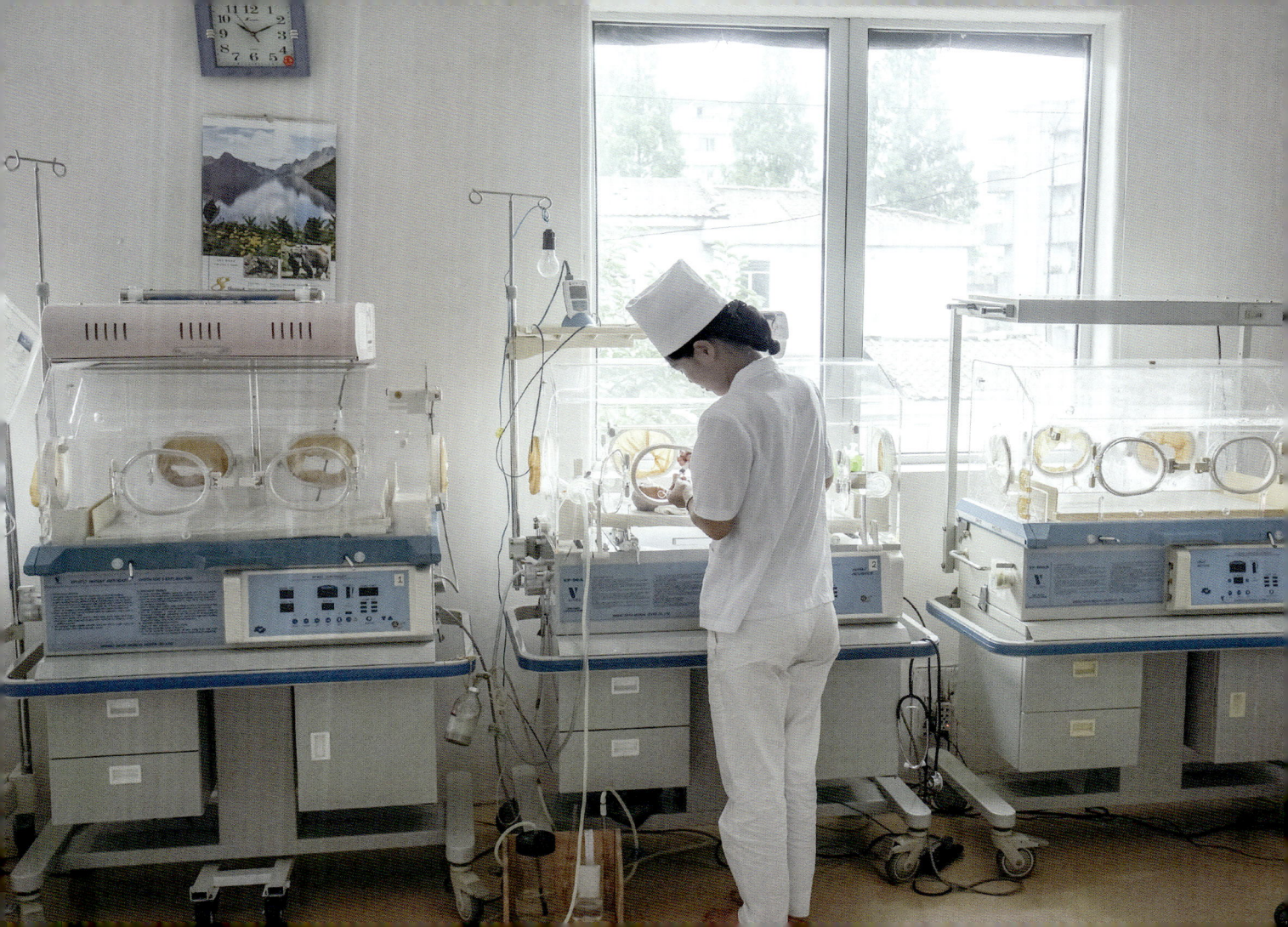

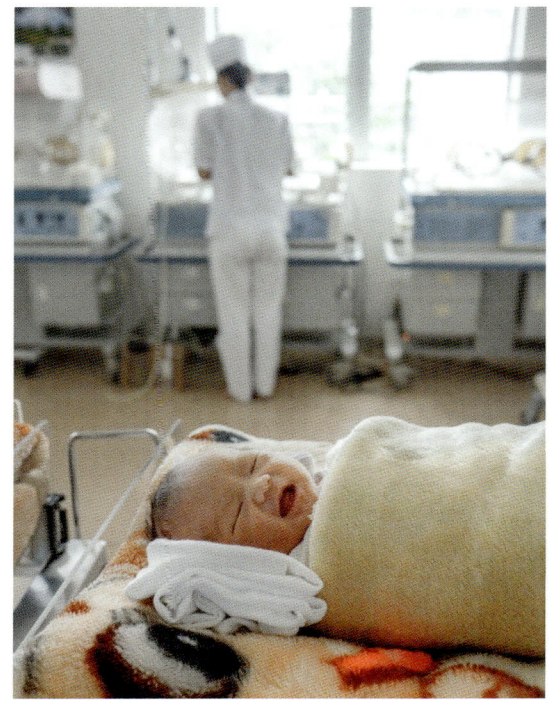
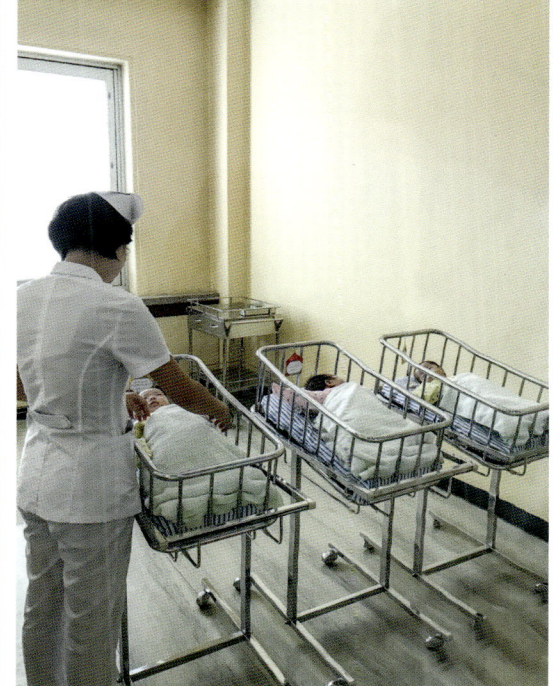

413-414 Ministering to a newborn baby in intensive care at Pyongyang Maternity Hospital. (2012)

평양산원 중환자실에서 신생아를 돌보고 있다.

415 A set of triplets. (2018)

세쌍둥이.

416 Administering physiotherapy, Academy of Traditional Korean Medicine. (2013)

물리치료, 고려의학대학 (한의대).

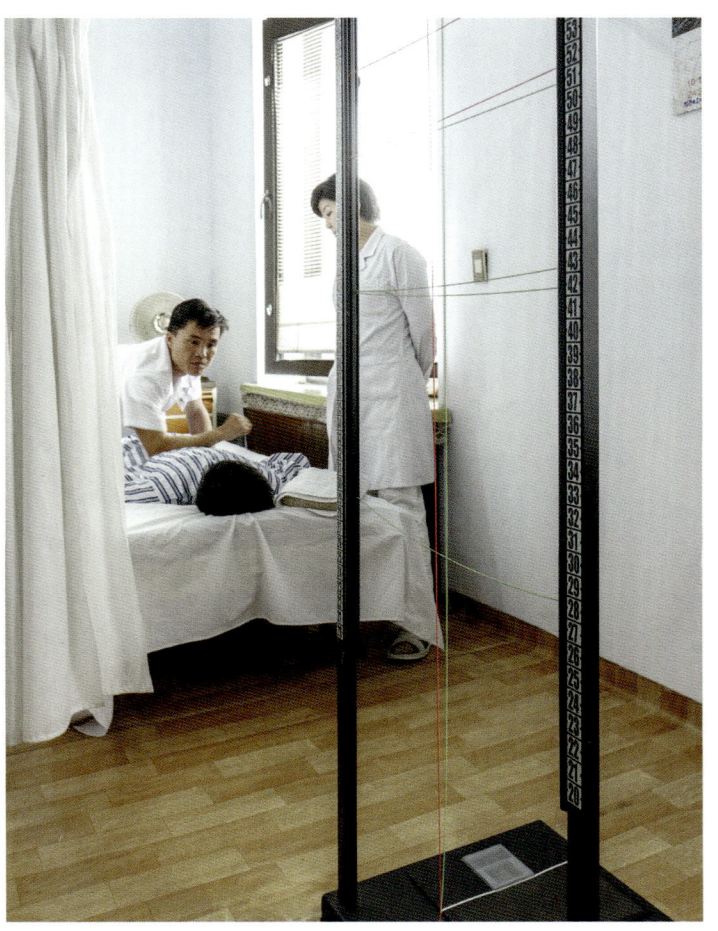

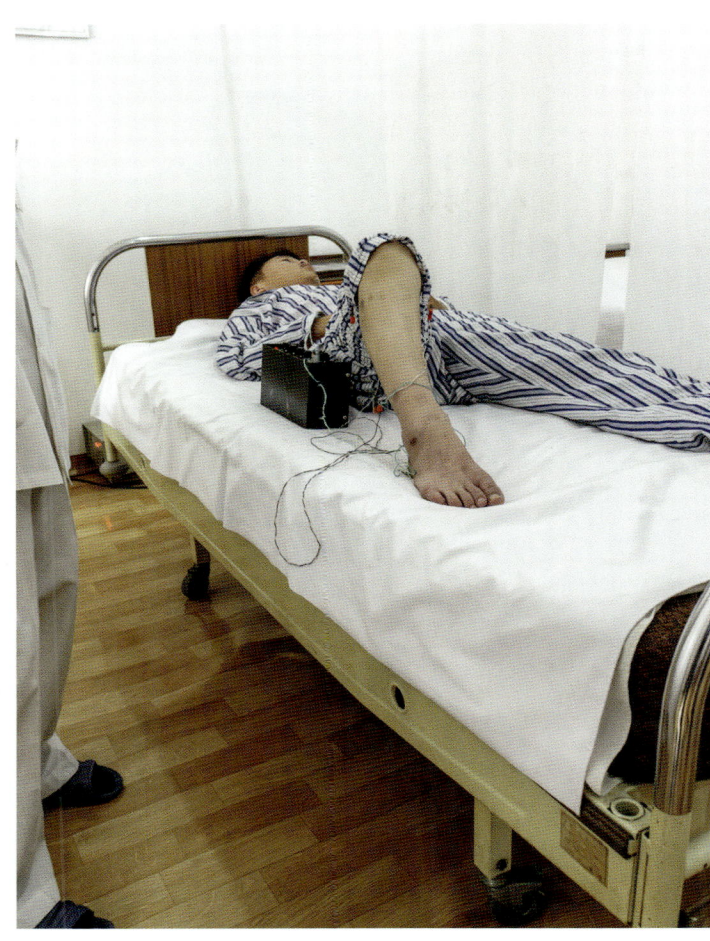

417 Plugged in patient.
의료기구 이용 환자.

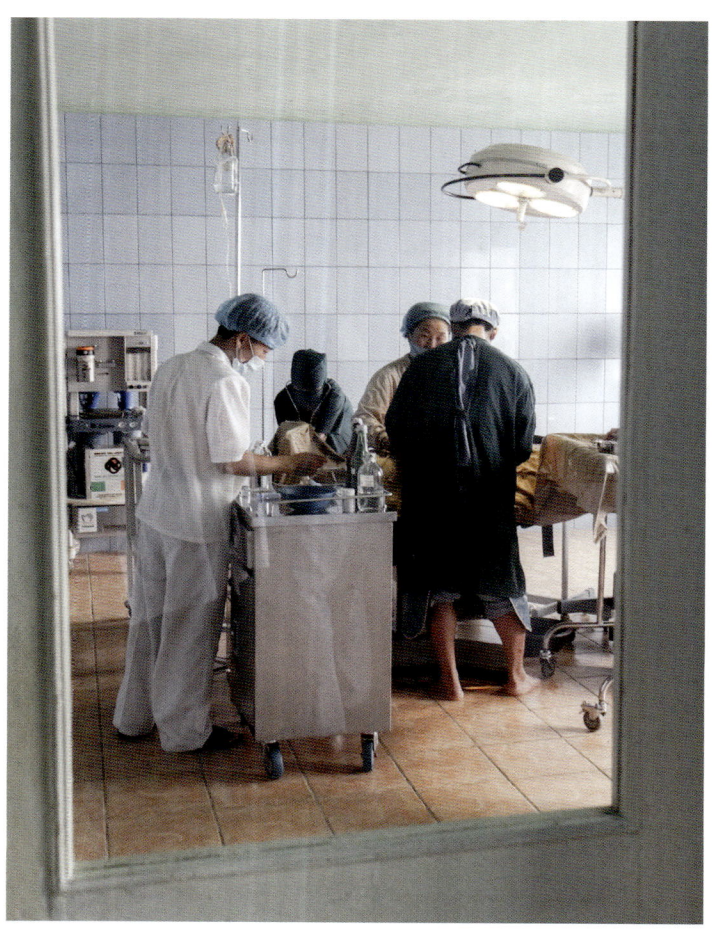

418 *Left* - 'Barefoot Doctor' operating in Pyongyang Hospital depicting aseptic technique. (2012)

좌 – 평양병원 '맨발의 의사'가 무균술을 보여주며 수술 중.

419 *Right* - Dental work. (2007)

우 – 치과 진료.

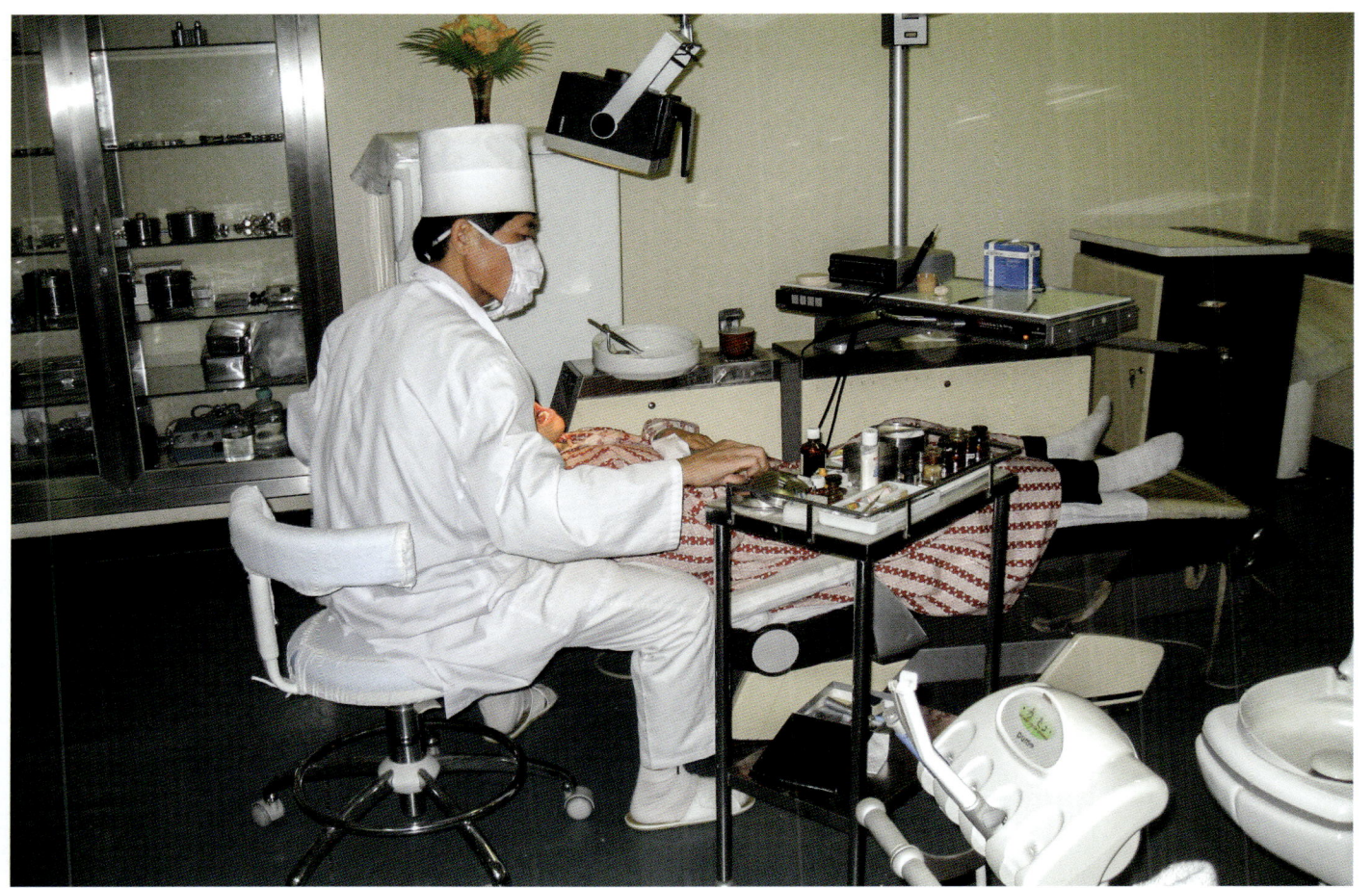

420 Pyongyang Maternity Hospital Director. (2011)
평양산원 원장.

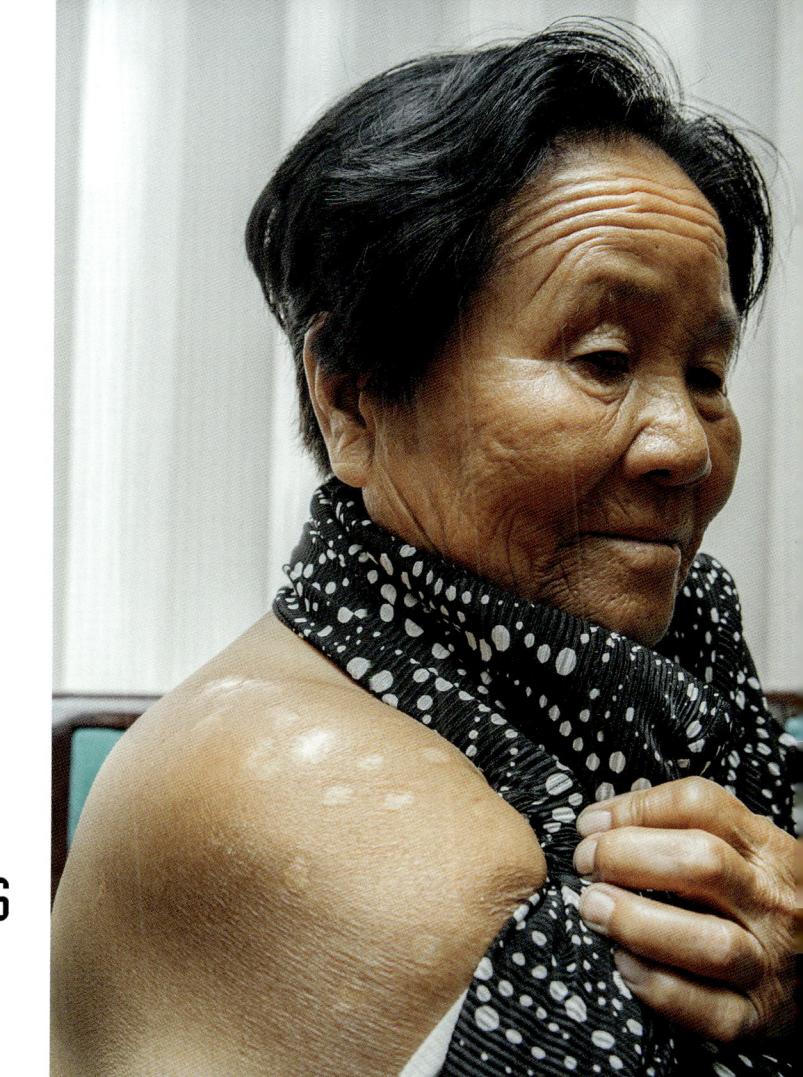

Personalities
인물

501   *Previous page* - Kim Yong Su, born 1926. One of the last of Japan's 'comfort women' in the North. Forced into prostitution during the Pacific War when little more than a child. She shows the scars from the cigarette burns she was forced to endure. © 2008 Irina Kalashnikova

전 페이지 - 김용수, 1926년생. 북한의 마지막 생존 일본군 '위안부' 중 한 명. 아직 어린아이에 지나지 않는 나이에 태평양전쟁 중 강제로 매춘을 해야 했던 그녀는 자신이 겪은 담뱃불로 지진 자국을 보여주고 있다. © 2008 이리나 칼라시니코바

502   *Right* - American defector James Dresnok, a US soldier who crossed the line to the North in 1962, with Irina Kalashnikova. Dresnok, who died in 2016, featured as the 'evil' American in the North's drama series *Unsung Heroes*. (2008)

우 – 1962년 월북한 미군 탈주병 제임스 드레스녹, 이리나 칼라시니코바와 함께. 2016년 사망한 드레스녹은 북한 드라마 '이름 없는 영웅들에서 '사악한' 미국인으로 출연했다.

503 *Left* - Two of the Japanese Red Army Faction Yodogo hijackers, who in March 1970, tried to divert a domestic flight to Cuba to undergo military training, Konishi Takahiro (L) and Wakabayashi Moriaki(R). Wakabayashi was the bass player with Japan's noise rock band Les Rallies Désnudés. With the plane lacking the range to reach Havana, they ended up being offered political asylum in Pyongyang. © 2008 Irina Kalashnikova

좌 - 1970년 3월 군사훈련을 받기 위해 일본 국내선을 쿠바로 돌리려 했던 일본 적군파 요도호 납치범 중 두 명인 고니시 다카히로(좌)와 와카바야시 모리아키(우). 와카바야시는 일본 노이즈 록 밴드 Les Rallies Désnudés의 베이스 연주자였다. 비행기의 항속거리가 하바나까지 미치지 못했으므로 그들은 결국 평양에서 정치적 망명을 제공받았다. © 2008 이리나 칼라시니코바

504 *Right* - Pak In Ho was the first to board the National Security Agency's *USS Pueblo* when it was captured off Wonsan in 1968. He served as a guide to the ship when it was moved and sailed around the Korean Peninsula to the Taedong river, Pyongyang in 1999. It was moved again in 2012 to the grounds of the Fatherland Liberation Museum, Pyongyang. (2009)

우 – 박인호는 미국 국가 안보국 정찰선USS 푸에블로호가 1968년 원산 앞바다에서 나포됐을 때 처음 승선한 인물이다. 그는1999년 배를 움직여 한반도를 돌아 평양 대동강까지 항해할 때 길잡이 역할을 했다. 푸에블로호는 2012년 다시 평양 조국해방전쟁승리기념관 부지로 옮겨졌다.

505 Two of the South's long-term prisoners held incognito. U Yong-Goo (L) who served 41 years was captured with the last of the partisans in 1958, while Hong Myong-Gil (R) served 38 years after being detained in 1960 as leader of the underground Revolutionary Party for Re-unification. © 2008 Irina Kalashnikova

남한에서 익명 장기수였던 두 사람. 우용구(좌)는 1958년 마지막 빨치산 대원들과 함께 잡혀 41년간 복역했고, 홍명길(우)은 1960년 지하조직 통일혁명당 두목으로 수감돼 38년간 복역했다. © 2008 이리나 칼라시니코바

Planes, Boats, and Trains
비행기, 배, 기차

601   *Previous page* - Beijing - Pyongyang train in the North. (2011)

전 페이지 – 베이징-평양간 열차.

602-603   Pyongyang Sunan airport before and after renovation. (2007 and 2014)

평양 순안공항의 개축 전고- 후의 모습.

604 *Left* - Air Koryo Flight Attendant promoting Ginseng. (2018)

좌 - 인삼을 홍보하는 고려항공 승무원.

605 *Right* - Moranbong Band, the country's most famous band, as in-flight entertainment. (2014)

우 - 기내 오락 프로로 제공되는 북한에서 가장 유명한 모란봉 밴드의 공연.

606 Car use is low but rising. Travelling by bike, which are licensed, is the most popular form of transport in the cities. (2009)

자동차 사용은 적지만 늘고 있는 중. 면허증이 발급되는 자전거가 도시에서 가장 인기 있는 교통 수단이다.

607 (2012)

608 Kim Jong Il was opposed to women riding bikes. In the cities, at least, it was close to forbidden between 1996 and 2012. Wonsan. (2013)

김정일은 여자들이 자전거 타는 것을 반대했다. 적어도 도시에서는 1996년에서 2012년까지 그것이 거의 금지됐다. 원산.

609 Advertisment for the Hwiparam II produced under licence by North Korean car manufacturer, Pyeonghwa. (2012)
북한 자동차 제조업체 평화가 라이선스 하에 생산한 휘파람 II 광고판.

610 Out of fuel. Pyongyang station, Sosong Street, opposite the Koryo Hotel. (2008)

연료가 떨어짐. 평양역, 서성거리, 고려호텔 맞은편.

611 Traffic police. Pyongyang's famous women live traffic lights go mixed outside of the capital. Kaesong city is about the only Northern city with traditional pre-war buildings extant. The city was below the 38th Parallel and as 'South Korean', escaped the US blanket bombing. (2009)

교통 경찰. 평양에는 유명한 여성 교통경찰들이 있지만 수도를 벗어나면 남녀 경찰이 섞여 있다. 개성시는 북한에서 전쟁 전의 전통적인 건물들이 남아있는 유일한 도시이다. 이 도시는 38선 아래 "남한" 지역에 놓여 있어 미국의 전면 폭격을 피해갔다.

612 At 'Mini-Korea' the red placard on the electric shuttle-bus indicates it was used previously by Kim Jong Un. (2012)

'미니 코리아'에 있는 전기 셔틀버스의 빨간색 표지는 이전에 김정은이 그 차를 사용했음을 나타낸다.

613 Army Soundtruck. 군 확성기 트럭.

614 *Left* - Taxi driver waiting for a customer. (2014)

좌 – 손님을 기다리는 택시 기사.

615 *Right* - Not everyone has the skills for winter driving. The highway to Sunan airport. (2017)

우 - 겨울 운전은 아무나 할 수 있는 게 아님. 순안 공항으로 가는 고속도로.

616 *Left* - With fuel scarce and expensive, many rural lorries have been converted to run on wood. They are not allowed within Pyongyang city limits. (2013)

좌 – 차 연료가 부족하고 비싸기 때문에 많은 시골 트럭들은 장작을 태워 운행하도록 개조되었다. 그런 차들은 평양시 경계 안에서는 허용되지 않는다.

617 *Right* - Petrol stations are few and far between, with additional petrol carried in cans in the boot. Near Wonsan. (2012)

우 - 주유소는 아주 드물고 서로 멀리 떨어져 있기 때문에 휘발유를 담은 캔을 별도로 차 트렁크에 싣고 다닌다. 원산 근처.

618 *Left* - The narrow-gauge train between Hungnam and Hamhung built during the Japanese occupation. (2012)

좌 -일제 강점기에 건설된 흥남-함흥 간 협궤열차.

619 *Right* - (2011)

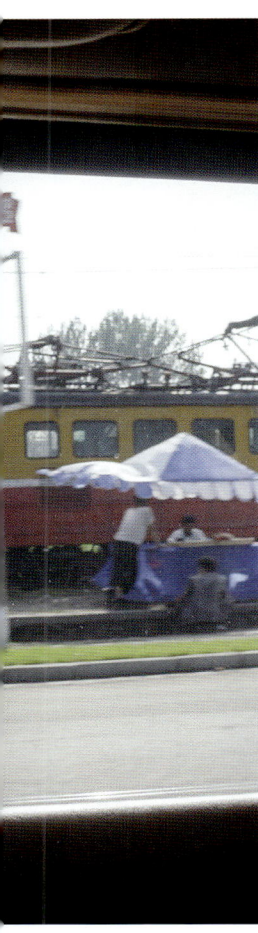

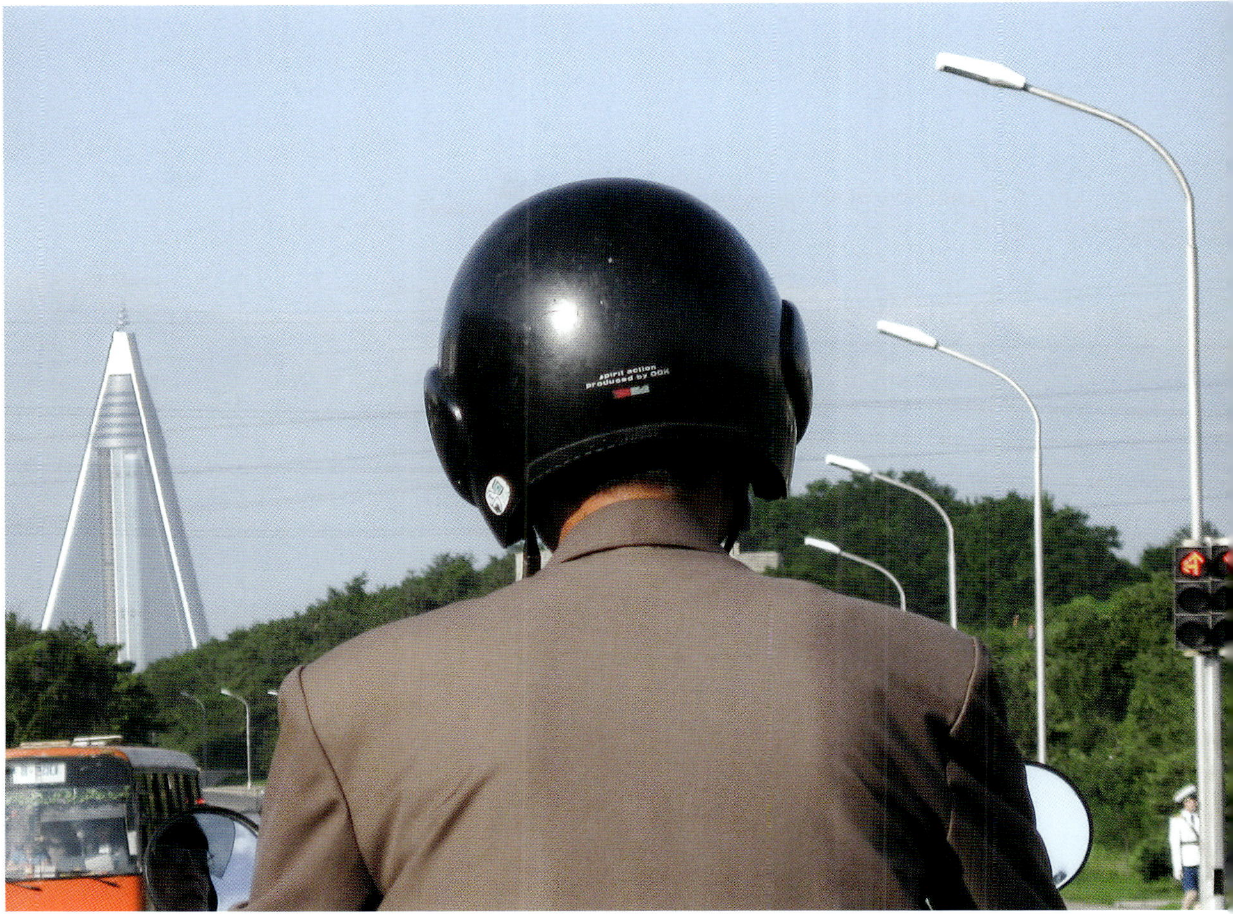
spirit action
produced by OOK

620 Heroic bus - each star represents 50,000km. This bus has driven more than 1,400,000km. (2012)

영웅적 버스 – 별 하나는 주행거리 5만km를 나타낸다. 이 버스는 140만km 이상을 주행했다.

621 Commuters reading *Rodong Sinmun* in Puhung Metro station. (2018)

지하철 부흥역에서 통근자들이 로동신문을 읽고 있다.

622 *Left* - Waiting to board. (2012)

좌 – 지하철을 타려고 기다리는 중.

623 *Right* - Signalling it's safe to depart. Open in 1969, the rolling stock was originally Chinese, but replaced by stock from the East German U-Bahn. Currently there are two lines with 16 stations over 22km. Each trip costs half a cent, making it the world's cheapest. (2011)

우 - 출발해도 안전하다는 신호를 보낸다. 1969년에 운행 개시된 지하철의 차량은 원래 중국제였지간 동독 지하철 차량으로 대체되었다. 현재 두개 노선에 운행 거리는 22km이상으로 16개 역이 있다. 요금은 한번 타는데 0.5센트로 세계에서 가장 저렴하다.

624 Sightseer boats in Rason waiting to take passengers to Pipha island to see dolphins. (2013)

돌고래를 보러 비파섬으로 갈 승객을 라선에서 기다리고 있는 유람선.

625 Rason port on pause as it waits to tranship coal from Russia and China to South Korea. (2013)

라선항이 한국으로 가는 러시아와 중국산 석탄을 환적하기 위해 대기 중이다.

626 Rascn sailors off Rajin Port. (2013)

라진항의 라선 선원들.

627　Boats on the DPRK bank of the Yalu River near Sinuiju. (2012)
　　　압록강 신의주 근처 북한측 둑에 있는 선박들.

628 Wonsan. (2013)
원산.

Rest and Play
휴식과 오락

701   *Previous page* - Munsu Water Park. (2013)
전 페이지 – 문수물놀이장.

702   On the beach. (2012)
해변에서.

703 Tattoos are a rare sight, generally limited to ex-military.
문신은 드물며 주로 전직 군인들만 한다.

706 Netball Practice. (2013)
네트볼 연습.

705 Songdowon beach, Wonsan. (2012)
송도원 해변에서 물놀이하는 어린이들, 원산.

707 Pyongyang Dolphinarium. (2011)
평양곱등어관(돌고래쇼공연장).

708 Sunrise Coffee. (2013)
선라이즈 커피.

709-710 Work day out. Rungrado Funfair. (2011)

직장야유회, 능라도 놀이공원.

711 Kaeson Youth Funfair. (2011)
개선청년공원.

712 *Left* - Kaeson Youth Funfair, completed 1984, renovated 2010. Visitors are 'work units' rewarded for their endeavours, topped up by those willing and able to pay the entrance fee. In the background is the 1982 Arch of Triumph celebrating victory in the 'Anti-Japanese Armed Struggle'. (2011)

좌 - 개선청년공원. 1984년 준공, 2010년 보수. 직장 단위 포상 휴가객들에 입장료를 낼 의사와 여유가 있는 방문객들이 합류. 뒤에 항일 무장독립투쟁 승리를 기념해 1982년에 건립된 평양개선문이 보인다.

713 *Right* - Fairground fast food.

우 - 공원 식품점.

714 Pyongyang Fast Food. (2014)
평양의 속성음식(패스트푸드).

715-717 Central Zoo which contains a Natural History Museum. Renovated in 2016. (2016)

조선중앙동물원에는 자연사박물관도 들어있다. 2016년 보수.

718-719 Hanging on the telephone, Mirim Riding School. (2013)

지금은 통화중, 미림승마구락부.

720-721 *Previous page* - A Star is born. Mass Games, May Day Stadium (2011)

전 페이지 - 북한 매스게임단이 별 모양을 만들고있다.

722-723 The Mass Games is world's largest gymnastic performance with over 100,000 participants.

집단체조(매스게임)는 10만명 이상이 참여하는 세계 최대 규모 공연.

724 When the show is over. (2012)
공연 후 풍경.

725 Pyongyang Gold Lane bowling. (2011)
평양보링관.

726 *Left* - DPRK Taekwondo. North and South each have their own Federations with no mutual recognition. (2011)

좌 - 북한 태권도. 남북한은 각자 서로 인정하지 않는 연맹을 갖고 있다.

727 *Right* - Kim Il Sung University. (2016)

우 - 김일성 대학.

728-729 Skate Park with the Kimilsungia and Kimjongilia Exhibition Hall in the background. (2013)

롤러스케이트장, 김일성화김정일화전시관이 뒤에 보인다.

730   Kim Il Sung Stadium. (2011)
김일성 경기장.

731 Korean People's Army plays Korean State Railway; April 25th beats Kigwancha 1-0.

4월 25일 조선인민군이 철도팀과의 축구 경기에서 기관차팀에 1-0으로 승리.

732 DPRK football kit. (2014)
북한 축구 꿈나무들.

733 Japanese 'Muji' store in the Ryomyong Street complex. (2017)

려명거리 복합단지 내의 일본 '무지' 매장.

734-735 Masikryong Ski Resort. (2018)
마식령 스키장.

736   Lunch in the Koryo. (2012)
고려식당에서의 오찬.

737 Taedonggang Beer Festival and the first beer to be advertised on Korean Central Television. © 2016 Chiara Zannini

대동강맥주 축제, 조선중앙TV에 최초로 광고된 맥주이다. © 2016 키아라 자니니

738 Lake Sijong health resort and its healing mud.
© 2008 Irina Kalashnikovav

시중호 요양소의 진흙 치료(2008) 사진제공: 이리나 칼라시니코바

739 High heels to the beach. Wonsan. (2013)
하이힐 신고 해변 나들이, 원산.

740 Street Gambling. (2012)
길거리 도박.

741 *Left* - Fighter fun. (1997)

좌 - 전투기 타기 놀이.

742 *Right* - Street volleyball beneath Juche Tower. (1997)

우 - 주체탑 아래서 길거리 배구.

743 (2011)

744-749 Manhwa mania (2001-2013)

만화마니아

744 *In the citadel of scheming*

745 *The identity of the white tiger*

746 *Human bullets*

747 *Long sword*

748 *Unshakable breakwater*

749 *They are back*

750 Hamhung Karaoke. (2011)
함흥 가라오케.

751 Wonsan's 'Japanese' restauranteur. (2013)
원산의 일식당 주인.

752 Mt. Kumgang guide. (2013)
금강산 안내원.

753 Mt. Myohyang picnic. (2016)
묘향산 소풍.

754　Package tour in Kumgang Mountains. (2013)
금강산 단체관광.

755 *Left* - Mt. Kumgang with tourists from the South before its closure in 2008 in the wake of a tragic death of a visitor. The building under construction was a Centre for North-South family re-unifications. (2007)

좌 - 2008년 한 관광객의 비극적 사망으로 폐쇄되기 이전에 남한 관광객들을 맞은 금강산 모습. 뒤에 남북이산가족면회소가 건축 중 이었다.

756 *Right* - Victorious Fatherland Liberation War Cemetery for those who died in 1950-53 and later. (2011)

우 - 6.25 전쟁 및 이후 전사자들을 위한 조국해방전쟁승리기념관.

Following up

While there is a wealth of material available in Korean about all facets of the DPRK, the same is less true in English. I would recommend my book Talking to North Korea: Ending the Nuclear Standoff (2018), also available in Korean.

The films of Nick Bonner:
Comrade Kim Goes Flying (2012). Directed by Kim Gwang Hun, Nicholas Bonner, and Anja Daelemans, UK.
Crossing the Line (2006) Directed by Koryo, Beijing.
The Game of Their Lives (2002). Directed by Koryo, Beijing.
A State of Mind (2004) Directed by Koyro, Beijing.

The music of Les Rallizes Desnudés – *Yoda-Go-A-Go-Go* and Laibach – *The Sound of Music*.

권장 추가 자료

북한에 대한 다각적 자료들이 한글로는 나와있지만 영어로는 그렇지 못하다. 나는 한국어로도 번역돼있는 내 저서 토킹 투 노스 코리아 - 우리는 북한을 정말 제대로 이해하고 있는가 (2018)를 권한다.

니콜라스 보너 영화:
김동무는 하늘을 날다 (2012).
니콜라스 보너, 김광훈, 안야 다엘레만스 감독, 영국.
푸른 눈의 평양 시민 (2006), 고려여행사, 베이징.
천리마 축구단 (2002), 고려여행사, 베이징.
어떤 나라 (2004), 고려여행사, 베이징.

Les Rallizes Desnudés 음악: Yodo-Go-A-Go-Go and Laibach – The Sound of Music.

Acknowledgements

First to Spencer Kim and everyone at the Pacific Century Institute. This would not have happened without him and them. Second to Tony Simpson and Spokesman for carrying the burden in the UK and EU. Will Devereux has done magic in giving life to tired old photographs from as long as a quarter of a century ago, while Irina Kalashnikova and Chiara Zannini have both allowed me to use photos taken while travelling with me in Pyongyang and beyond.

Marialaura De Angelis, Sonja Bachman, Munkhzul Bat-Erdene, Kent Härtstedt, Hyeyeon Holly Kang, Mary Sun Kim, Emma Leslie, Sam Martell, Tereza Nóvotna, Jonathan Powell, John Sagar, Mark Seddon and Michel Wood have all made their mark. I apologise to anyone I've missed. While my staff working with Track2Asia, in particular Guillermo Gallent Loria and Ilia Bekou, have suffered from my obsessions as have my long suffering family across generations. Thank you to KCNA for the author image on the back cover.

Despite this, the images and text remain the sole responsibility of the author.

감사의 말

제일 먼저 Spencer Kim과 Pacific Century Institute의 모든 분들께 감사드린다. 그들이 없었다면 이 작업은 이루어지지 않았을 것이다. 두 번째로 영국과 EU에서 고생해준 Tony Simpson 과 Spokesman에게 감사드린다. Will Devereux는 25년이나 지나 낡고 오래된 사진에 생명을 불어넣는 마법을 부렸고, 이리나 칼라시니코바와 키아라 자니니는 나와 함께 평양과 그 너머를 여행하면서 찍은 사진들을 사용할 수 있게 허락해줬다.

Marialaura De Angelis, Sonja Bachman, Munkhzul Bat-Erdene, Kent Härtstedt, Hyeyeon Holly Kang, Mary Sun Kim, Emma Leslie, Sam Martell, Tereza Nóvotna, Jonathan Powell, John Sagar, Mark Seddon, Michel Wood등 이들 모두가 중요한 기여를 했다. 내가 놓친 분들이 있으면 이 자리를 빌어 사과드린다. 또 Track2Asia와 일하는 우리 직원들, 특히 Guillermo Gallent Loria와 Ilia Bekou는 여러 세대에 걸친 내 가족이 오래 참아주었듯이 내 집착으로 인한 고통을 견뎌줬다. 뒷표지에 나오는 저자 사진을 제공해 준 조선중앙통신사에 감사드린다.

본서에 나오는 모든 사진과 글에 대한 책임은 오직 저자에게 있음.

English typeset using Industria for headings and Utopia for body of text.

Korean typeset using Source Han Sans KR for headings and Source Han Serif K for body of text.